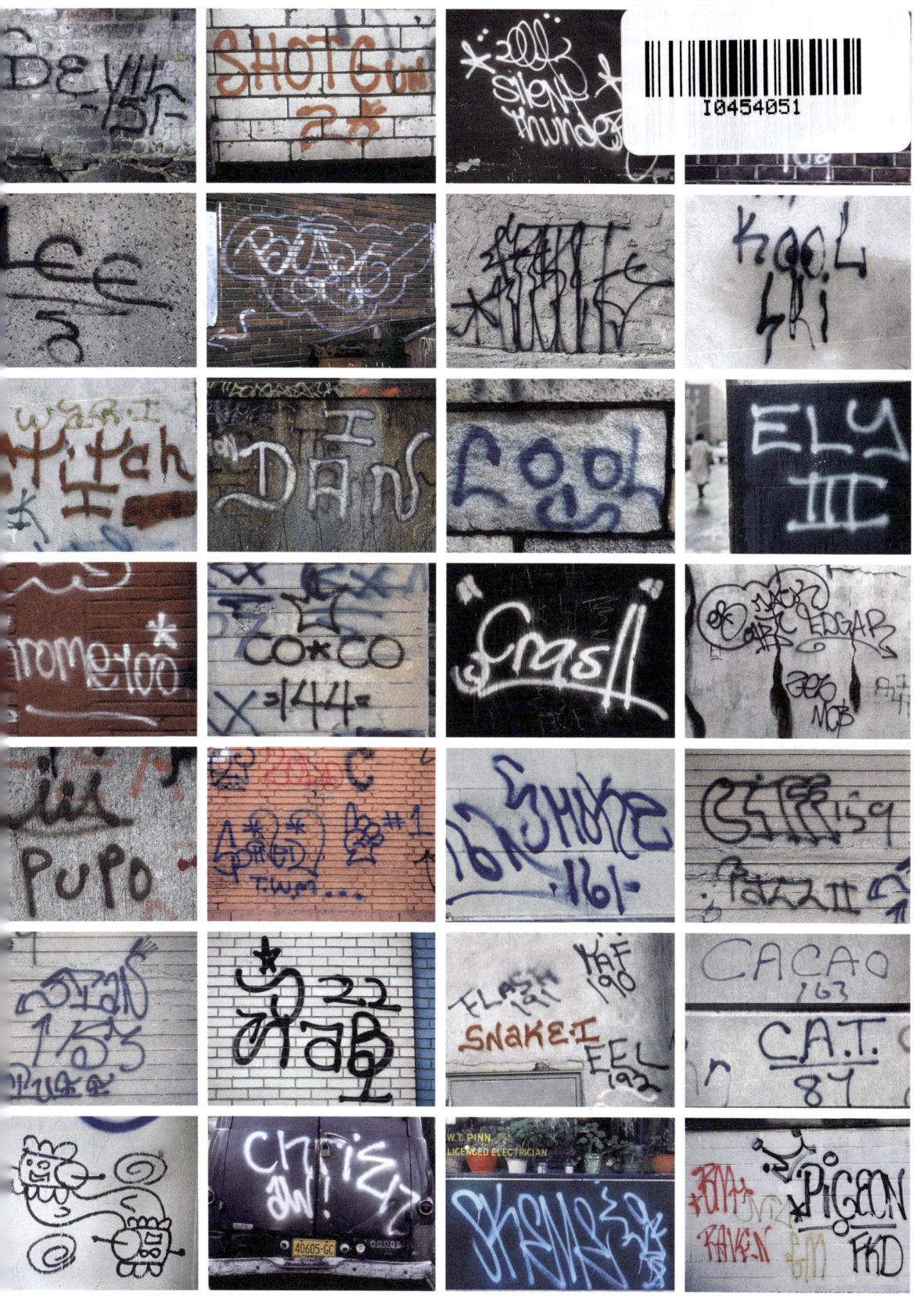

TAG TOWN

General stylistic Characteristics:
- backhand (slanting back or at least straight up & down)
- letters overlapping, compressed or touching, one line used for 2 letters as Æ
- unlabored, dashed off
- tendency to invert rounded letters & straight lines so in ÞD (eg. p's & d's) and AN
- often mixing upper & lower case

motifs, symbols —
- numerals - for street as in TAKI 183, for 1ˢᵀ to write name as in stitch I   ⎰Roman num. usually but not always⎱
  or for best as in minone.   Ⅱ (phase 2)
- stayhigh saint figure w. joint
- halo
- stars (over i, under exclam. ! + misc)
- quotation marks
- arrows
- arrows to heart ♡ ⬦
- crown
- copyright © or trademark ®
- cloud
- misc. 🎵 ⚥ ⌂ ⌂
- dots & periods C.A.T.
- anthropomorphic especially using OO names KOOL OO7 COOKIE
- exclamation point ♂ ♀ from
- s to dollars sign $
- ∞ pretzel twist as in Blade & Zephyr

pre + suffix —
Lady...   mr....   lil...
...ski   ...roc(k)   ...ster   ....ism   ....   / ...one ⌐

TAG TOWN

Martha Cooper

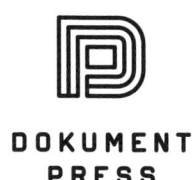

DOKUMENT
PRESS

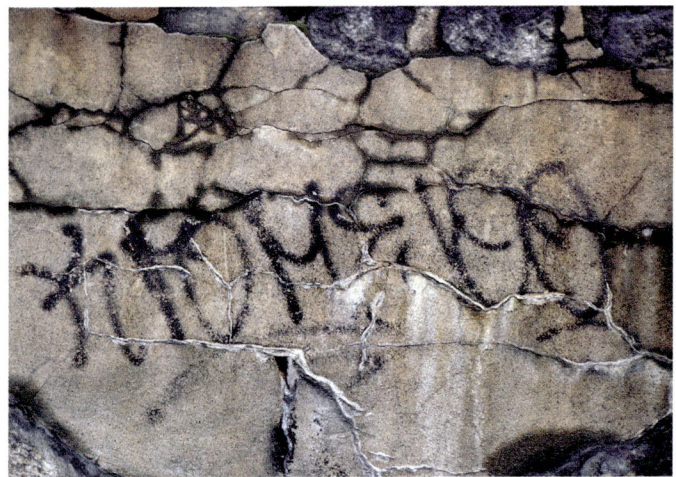

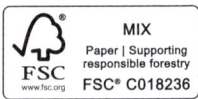

Photo & text: Martha Cooper
Cover photo: Smily
Photo p 2: Notes on tags, ca 1981
Photo p 76 by Crachee, courtesy of Blade
Photo p 108: The inside cover of
Martha Cooper's blackbook, early 1980s.
Text & graphic design: Tobias Barenthin Lindblad
Redesign for this edition: Martin Ander
Interviews with Part 1 and Snake 1: Jacob Kimvall
Translation from Swedish: Martin Thomson

Tag Town: The Evolution of New York
Graffiti Writing 1963–1982
Copyright © 2008, 2026 Dokument Press
First published in 2008 (paperback)
Second edition, first printing
Printed in Poland 2026
ISBN 978-91-89944-13-8

Dokument Press
Årstavägen 26, 120 02 Årsta, Sweden
www.dokumentpress.com
hello@dokumentpress.com

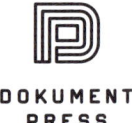

DOKUMENT PRESS

Content

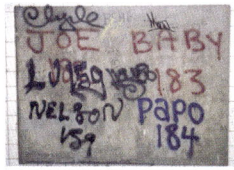
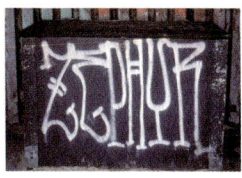
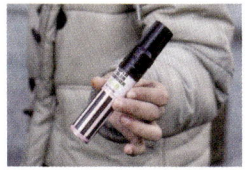
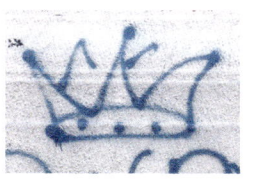
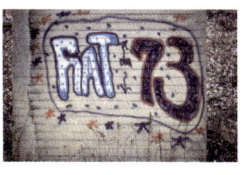
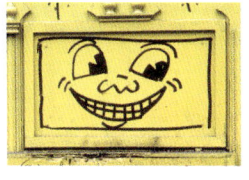
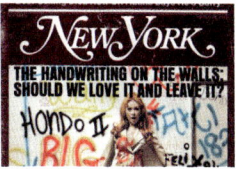

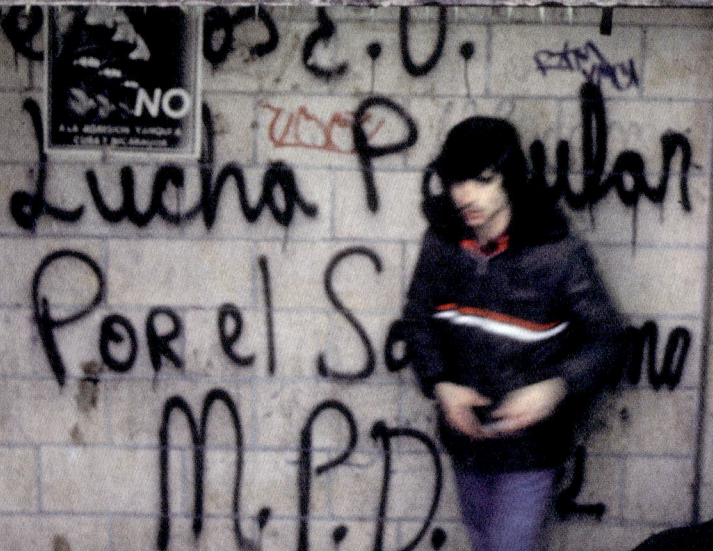

Foreword

In the beginning is The Name. You are given a name and become somebody; without a name you are no-one. Names give us the opportunity for immortality. To be deprived of one's name is an extreme punishment.

Writing one's name is to leave a part of oneself behind for all to see. Writing one's name consolidates one's identity. A president signs a document. A tag-writer signs his surroundings.

New York, 1970. The Vietnam war, a raging heroin epidemic, and a feeling of impending apocalypse. Despite the civil rights movements of the 60s, injustices persist. Police corruption is rife and youth gangs rule the streets.

With paint, youths find a fun and exciting alternative to violence and dejection. They develop a game of their own where they write a name – not their given name, but a street name – as stylishly and often as possible. The writer makes an advertisement, not to sell anything, but just for his own name.

Tags are *meaningless*. It is the user who fills them with content, meaning. Content is predicated by two parameters, quality and quantity. Writers write their tags wherever they can reach. Those who have talent are noticed for their style, and don't have to write as much to achieve fame.

It's impossible to tell who was first. There are early examples of almost-tags. Joseph Kyselak was an Austrian civil servant, who wrote his name all over the country in the 1820s. Like Kilroy Was Here – everywhere! Scrawling your name is a practice as old as time, and a tag is a name. The name is a means of exploring your neighborhood, and the whole town.

In gang war New York, writers pulled together, regardless of their background. "It ain't where you

from, it's where you at", as Rakim says in his song "I Know You Got Soul".

Many people think that Taki 183 from Washington Heights in Northern Manhattan was the first writer. In fact there were quite a few before him. We know that Cornbread, from Philadelphia, started tagging in 1965. But the Philadelphia scene never extended beyond the city's borders, although Top Cat 126 moved to New York in the early 70s, bringing with him a Philadelphia style that came to be known as Broadway Elegant. It was the New York graffiti movement that spread. It is this movement that all writers today, worldwide, are a part of.

Not everybody agrees on what constitutes a tag. What are the defining characteristics of tags in the New York City-tradition, that can be found all over the world? A tag is something that fits either or both of these criteria:

1. A tag is a logo in the form of an alias. It consists of letters and/or numbers (tags consisting only of numbers are rare, but do exist) and refers to one individual or a crew. The tag is a part of the New York graffiti tradition.

2. A tag forms part of a network of other tags, written in public space without permission. Location, frequency and aesthetics are the most important components.

Tags are most often styled, even though many early ones weren't. Some say that tags must be illegal to qualify. They forget all those written in blackbooks, on backpacks, closet doors, T-shirts and schoolbooks.

Tags aren't just the result of tagging. They also have an easily recognizable aesthetic that can be seen on clothing, in typography and art today.

Kyselak and Kilroy worked alone, but Taki's tags communicated with those of his friends. Writing your name was a game – who can get up the most? As a messenger Taki was one of the first to go all city.

For the non-initiated a tag mostly means nothing, while for the initiated it can be read like a hunter reads an animal's track in the forest: who passed here when, what were the circumstances? The initiated are able to read how a writer chooses to write, and where.

The general public recognized Taki's name, but didn't know what it meant or how to interpret it. His tags didn't communicate to most of them.

At 188th Street and Audubon Avenue in Washington Heights, writers found one of their first venues and called it Writers' Corner. Stitch 1 was the president. The youth gangs of New York and other big cities also wrote tags but mainly to mark the boundaries of their territory, like a homeowner erecting a fence. New York writers wrote their names all over town. They avoided gangs and moved across borders with greater freedom. Perhaps the graffiti movement even contributed to weakening the gangs in the mid 70s.

There are other interesting connections between tags and society. Tags became a mass movement at the same time as calligraphy enjoyed a renaissance in the us. Both movements can be seen as a reaction to depersonalization in the autobahn society, claims David McClelland (in his article reproduced on page 99). In that case, it is not the first time. Since the 19th century, it has been fashionable to collect your friends' signatures, accompanied with poems or punch lines, in little autograph books.

When Martha Cooper moved to Washington Heights in the early 80s, she had already begun to photograph graffiti. She realized that tags were names and was annoyed at the common perception that graffiti pieces were art but tags were vandalism. After failed efforts to design a tag of her own, she became convinced that tags required much practice to be eye-catching, recognizable and stylish.

In late 1981, when Martha began seriously to photograph tags, most of the early ones had already vanished. Old tags written in subways and in the streets had been painted over or faded away. But Martha lived in a gold mine. Washington Heights was an early hot spot for New York graffiti, and she started digging around for old tags herself. Bridge supports, parks, roofs and underpasses from the Bronx to Brooklyn were her Pompeii. Vintage tags were easy to identify. They looked naive and unpolished compared to the slick tags of today.

Surprisingly many old tags remained, but not in spite of the buff, as this did affect trains but not yet walls of buildings. It was only with the zero tolerance policy of the 1990s that cities in the Western World actively exterminated a century of handwriting from exteriors.

In the early 70s, tagging developed from neighborhood mischief into a citywide subculture. Writers soon discovered that a train written on in the yard rode all over town the next day. Communication moved faster. Subway graffiti is akin to an early version of the internet. The names of earlier generations of taggers were left to their fate in the cracks of New York.

Tag Town is not a catalog of who wrote the most. These are the tags that remained. Martha Cooper walked right into an archive, and this is a unique document of an age that has been erased.

It is often asserted that graffiti received a huge

boost through an interview with Taki 183 in the New York Times in the summer of 1971. Whether that article had a major impact or not is hard to say. What's important is that New York had a tagging scene long before 1971. Even if the dates are unverifiable, *Tag Town* includes tags dated as early as 1963.

In the article, Taki himself names Julio 204 as a predecessor. But nobody interviewed Julio about his influences. Someone inspired him; he must have seen even older tags. Some of his inspiration can be found in Herbert Kohl's excellent book *Golden Boy as Anthony Kool* which deals with the uptown scene prior to Taki. It is most likely that tagging was widespread in 1971, and that the Times article was an acknowledgement on the part of the adult world that graffiti was something to reckon with. For those in doubt, Check the 1966 Stevie Wonder LP *Down to Earth*. On the record jacket, Stevie is sitting on a stoop. Behind him is a freshly-styled tag: Joe 58.

Tags are a dialogue between the anonymous writer and the world around him. The tradition of name writing on walls is thousands of years old, and was carried on with relative openness until the early 70s. In 1972, New York mayor John Lindsay approved the first anti-graffiti law in the subway. He started a war on graffiti that all subsequent New York mayors have waged, with little success. The much discussed Broken Windows theory spread ten years later, planting the seed for the mid-90s zero tolerance policy. Zero tolerance policy in the West may be a consequence of Lindsay's efforts to halt graffiti.

The writer who has learned to master the basics develops personal touches that are easily recognizable but can also be "bitten". Give an experienced writer fifteen minutes, and he can copy most other tags. But tagging is a system based on a code – don't steal another person's style.

Today, the graffiti movement has grown up. In Europe, writers occasionally look back to the original styles, both for inspiration and as an attempt to approach the letters with a naïve view. All writers talk about their reaction to the first tags they saw. But it is impossible to regain that untrained eye. Once you have learned to read, you cannot return to illiteracy.

Observe someone writing a tag: angles at less than ninety degrees, long swooping lines, circles and loops. Concentration, rhythm, dance, writing. The writer feels the same pleasure in writing his tag again and again as does the Chinese calligrapher who repeats his characters, year after year. The small variations are endless. It is impossible to make exactly the same tag twice, and writing conditions affect both execution and result. Tags are a product of a highly developed culture, a society that has mastered written language. They are a new language, created on the street.

Tags are beautiful to those who have learned to read them. They open worlds of styles associated with various schools or writers around the globe. But as long as they are fought with zero tolerance, it seems that the general public's ability to enjoy their beauty is limited.

Painted trains still roll in cities around the world. Like music, tags are a universal language. With their rhythmic aesthetics, tags are the free jazz of lettering.

Tobias Barenthin Lindblad
Stockholm, Sweden

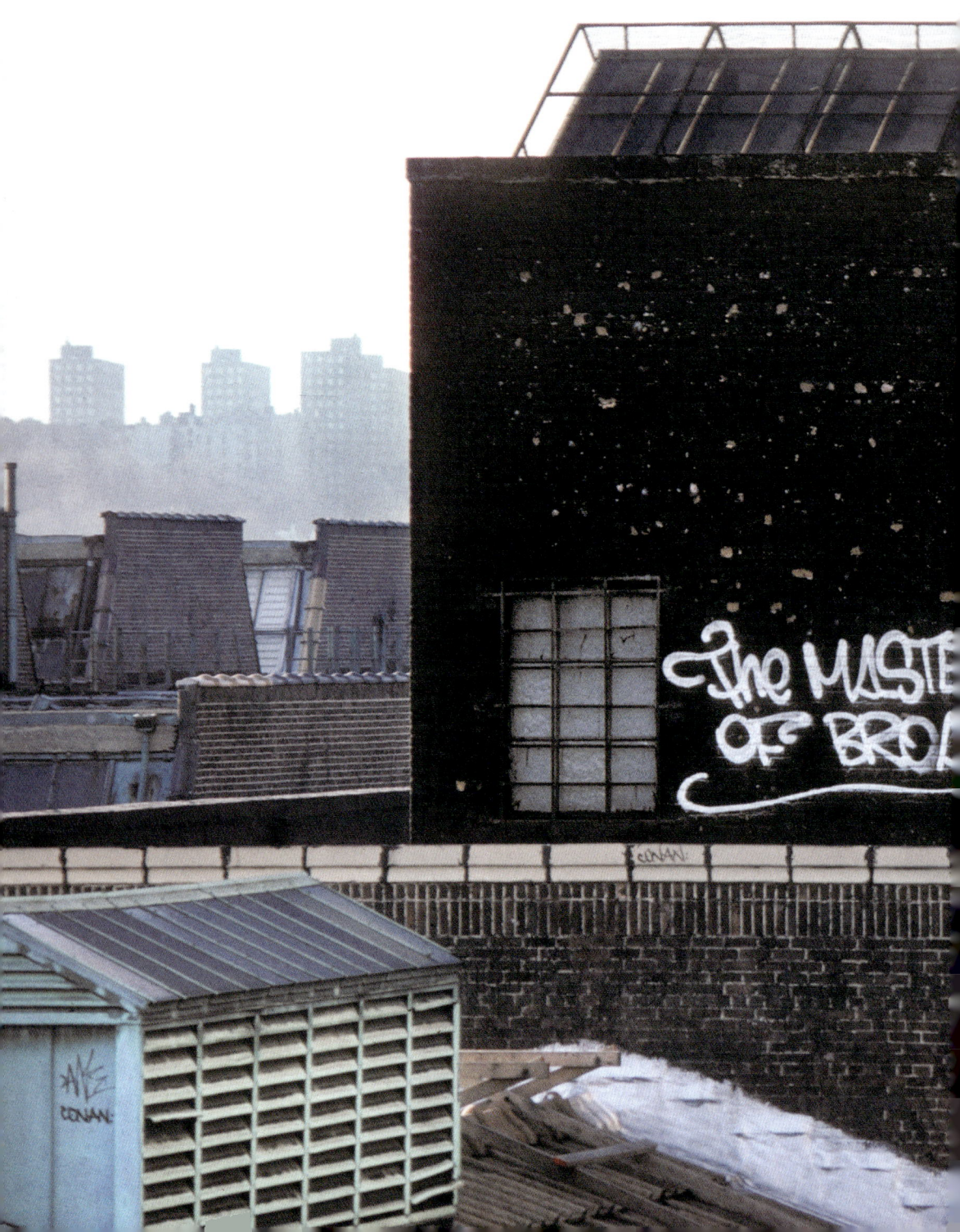

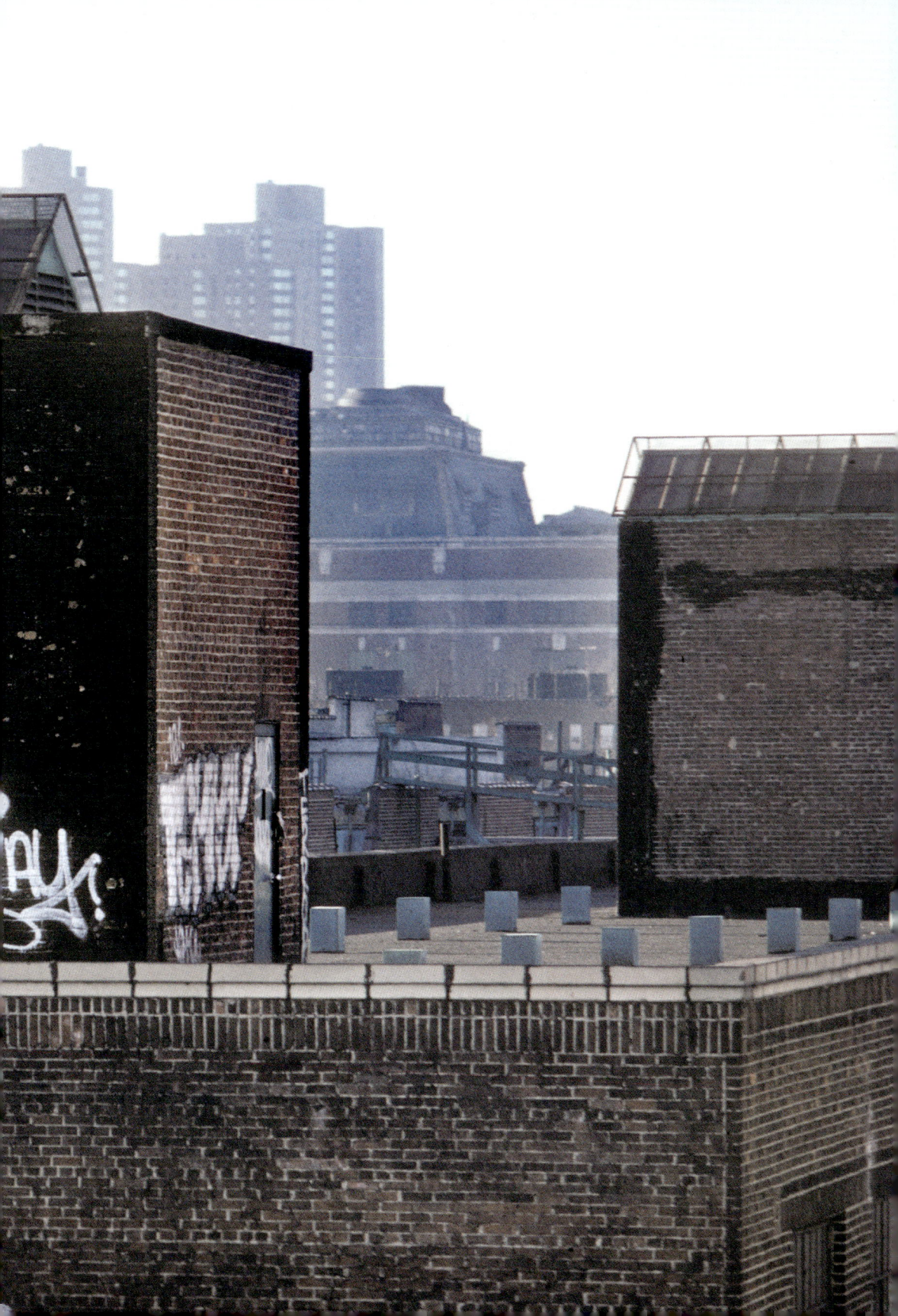

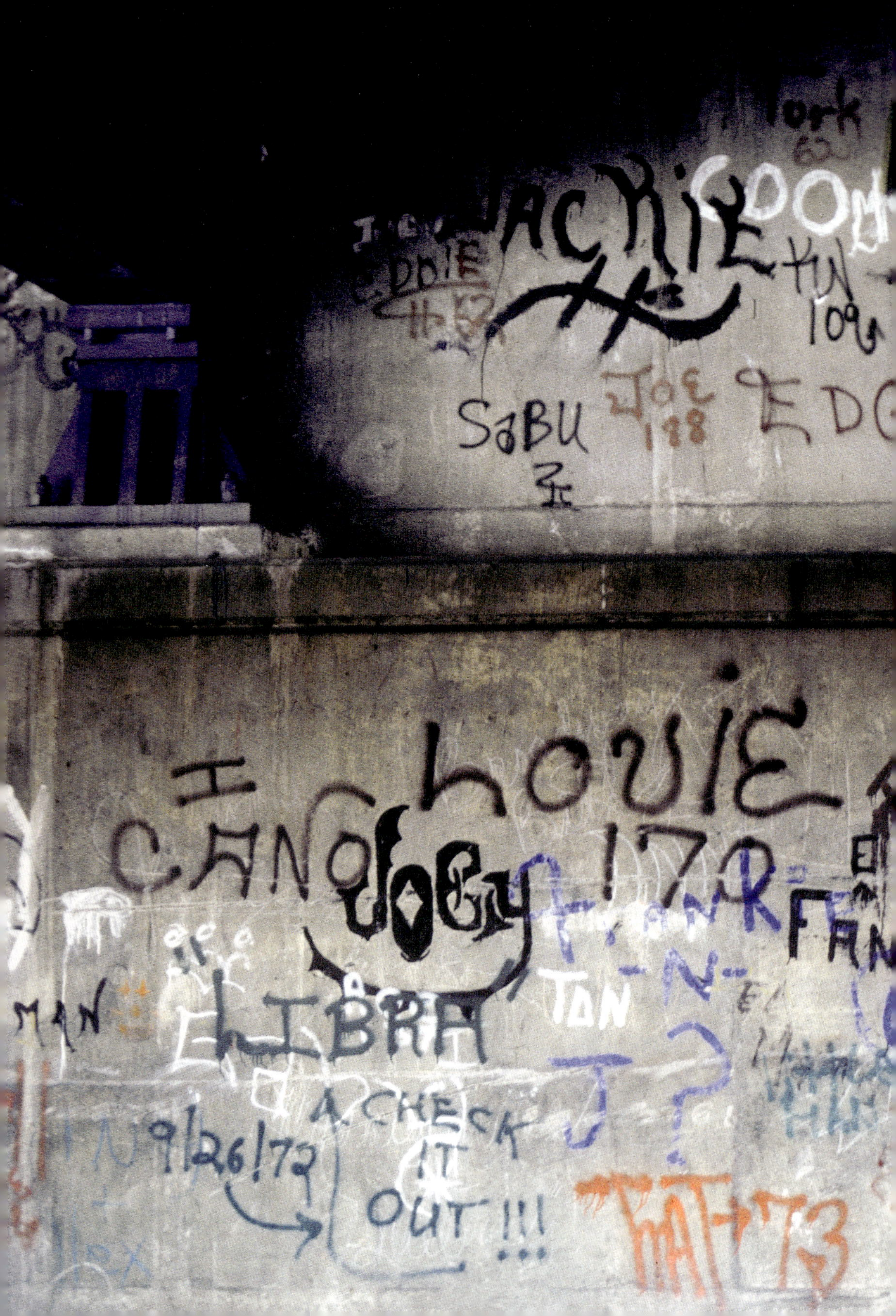

York 62

JACKIE DOM

EDDIE 153

TUN 109

SABU

JOE 88

EDG

hOViE 172

CANOLOGY JOGY

FAN

TON

MAN

LIBRA

A CHECK IT OUT !!!

IN 9|26|72

MAT 73

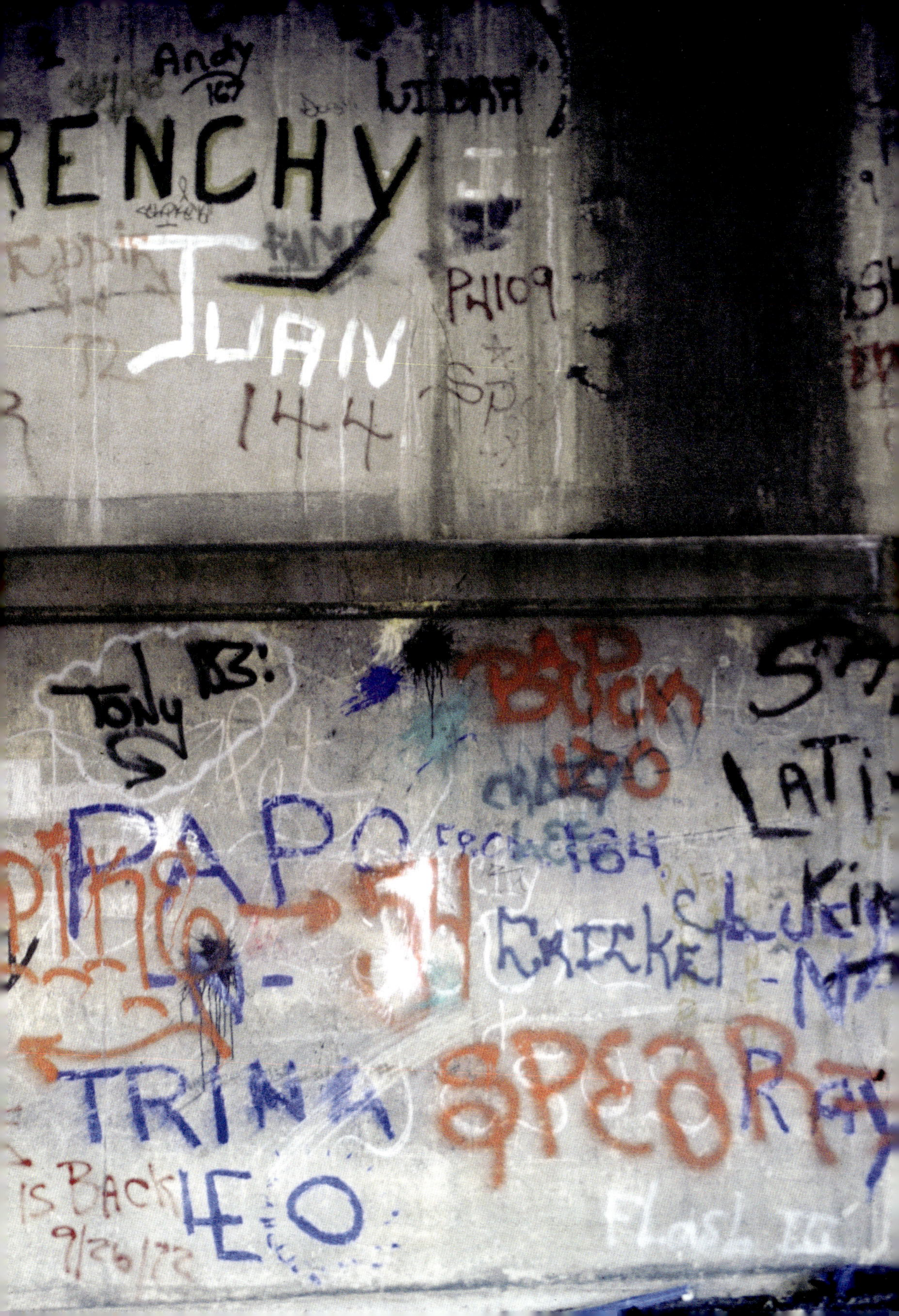

Andy
167
RENCHY
JUAN
144
TONY
DAPO
TRINA
LEO
is BACK
9/26/72
CRICKET
SPEAR
LATI

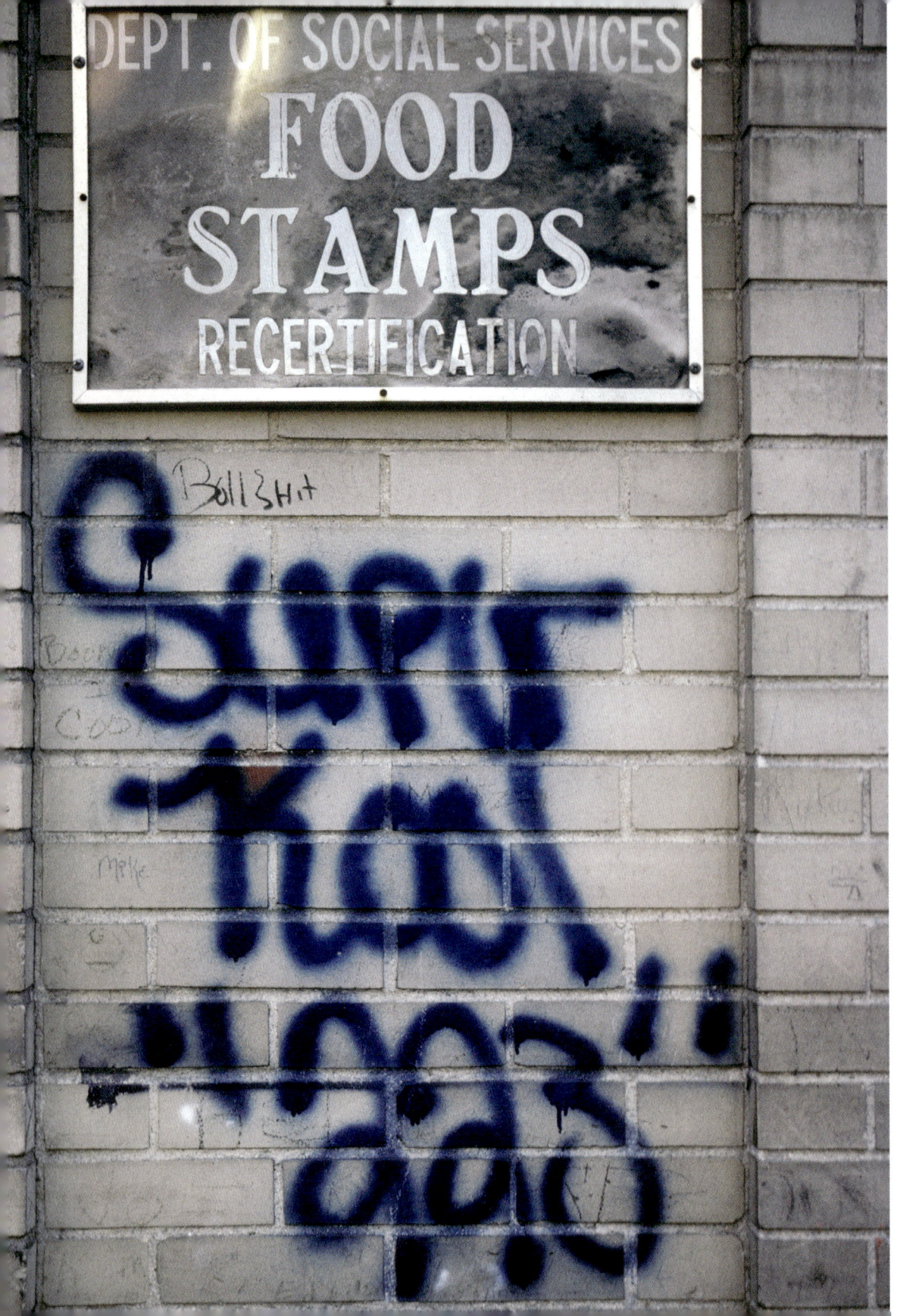

The Name

Developing an original, consistently written name is the primary act for a writer. In the 60s, kids wrote their given names or a nickname. Soon they began to use aliases, assuming names that both looked and sounded cool. Some borrowed and modified names from ads, comics, music and other popular culture.

Others invented names, used nicknames conferred by their friends or chose names simply because they liked the way the letters looked. Early writers added street numbers to their tags but later dropped them or changed them to throw the cops off their track.

At first, writers mostly tagged in their own neighborhoods. In 1971, the New York Times published an interview with Taki 183, a messenger who traveled and wrote his name all over the city. This article gave impetus to an already rising movement. Like an advertising campaign, the object of the game, was to get one's name up as many times as possible. The ultimate insult was to call someone a DGA, or *Don't Get Around*.

Blade fondly recalls walking with his partner Comet, along the FDR drive from midtown to the Bronx, a distance of about ten miles. They bought quarts of Colt 45 beer and "… hit every wall you could possibly hit. Blade-Comet – Blade-Comet – hundreds and hundreds of times!"

Longer names, such as Super Kool or Ultra Fly, eventually gave way to shorter names that were quicker to write, such as Snake or Blade. Originality

was prized and using the same name as another writer was disparaged as biting. One way writers protected their names from biting was by adding the Roman numerals I and II. Snake I used to add *King of all Snakes. Ya dig!* after his name because there were so many other Snakes.

Girls also wrote, and the pioneers, Barbara 62, Eva 62 and Charmin 65, are graffiti legends. Boys some-times wrote their girlfriends' nicknames, or vice versa. Crews of writers formed and kids added those names or initials to their own tags. Ex Vandals was the first organized group of writers in 1971 and heavily influenced future crews.

Tagging in unusual or outrageous places was another way to get fame. Snake and his friends Stitch 1, Web 2, and Cat 87 once tagged the windshield of a bus while the driver dozed inside. Another time Snake and Stitch hit parked cop cars in front of the precinct with markers and the side of the precinct building with Red Devil, Regal Blue spray paint. But during one tagging spree, Snake, Stitch 1 and Spanky 132 were caught in the act.

"The cops took our spray paint away, made us turn around and painted the back of our jackets with P.D." Unfortunately Snake was wearing a brand new leather jacket.

Tagging is both competitive and fun. While writers claim to be bold and ruthless in their writing, their chief goal is an aesthetic presentation of their name.

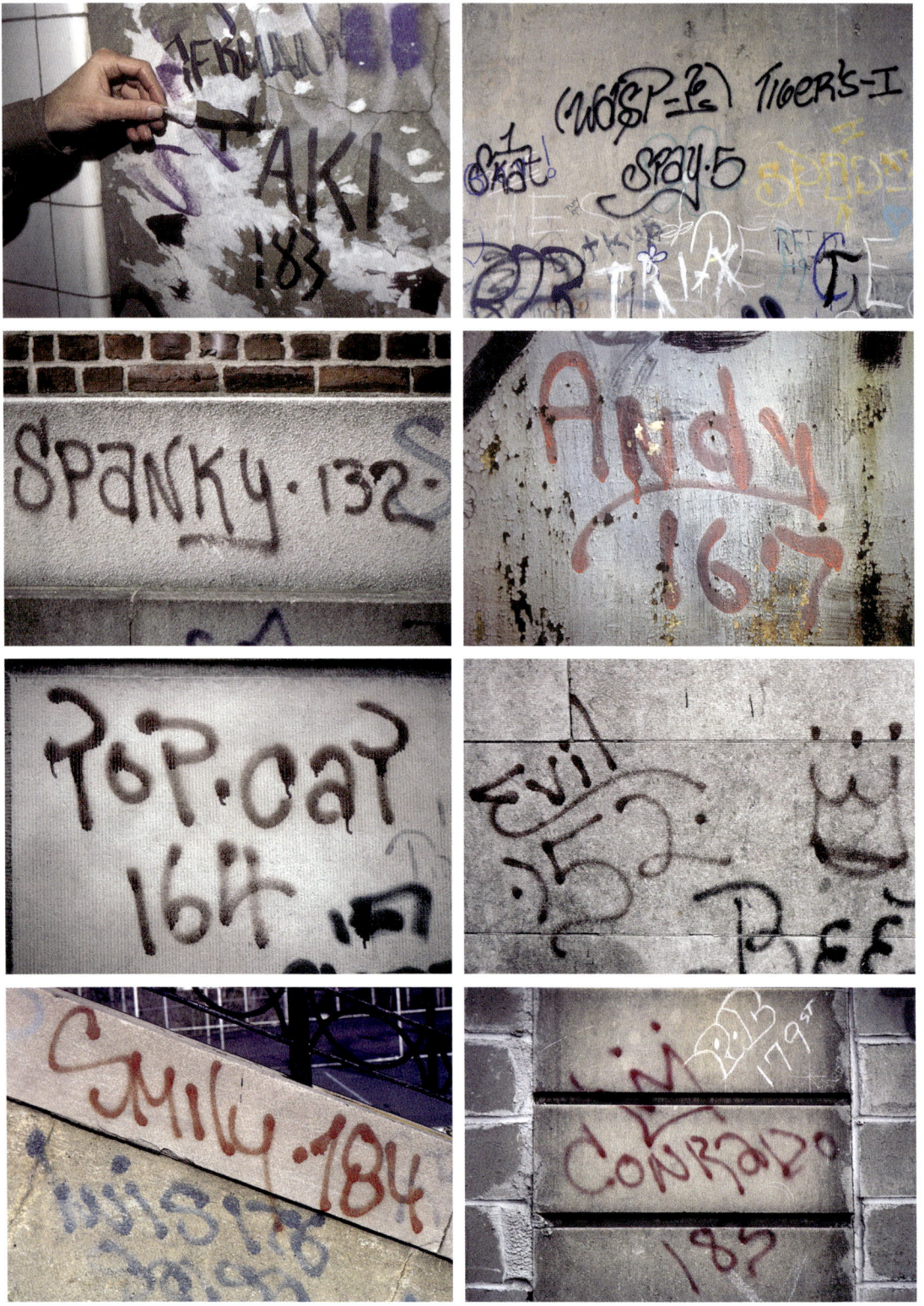

The Name – Street Numbers

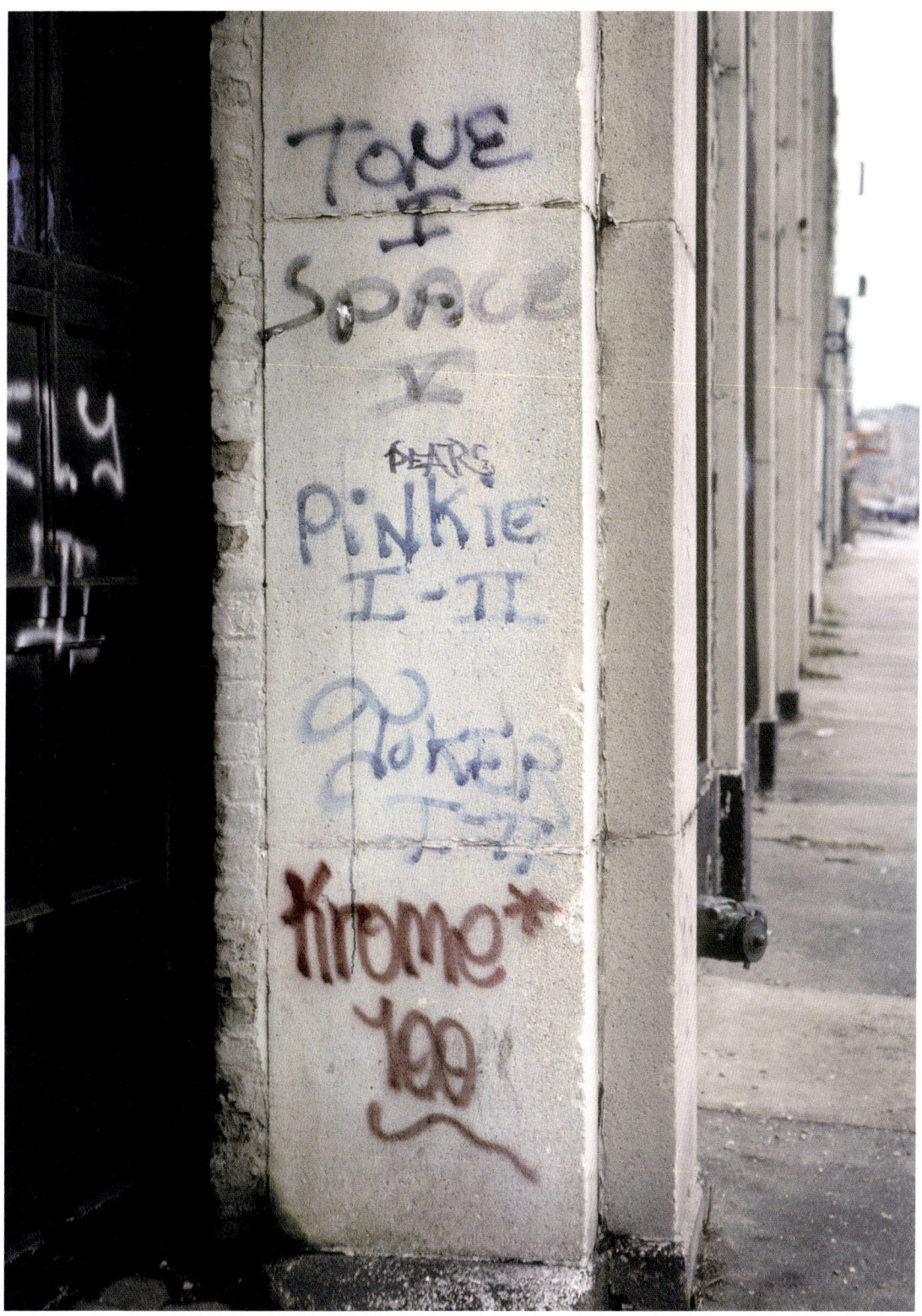

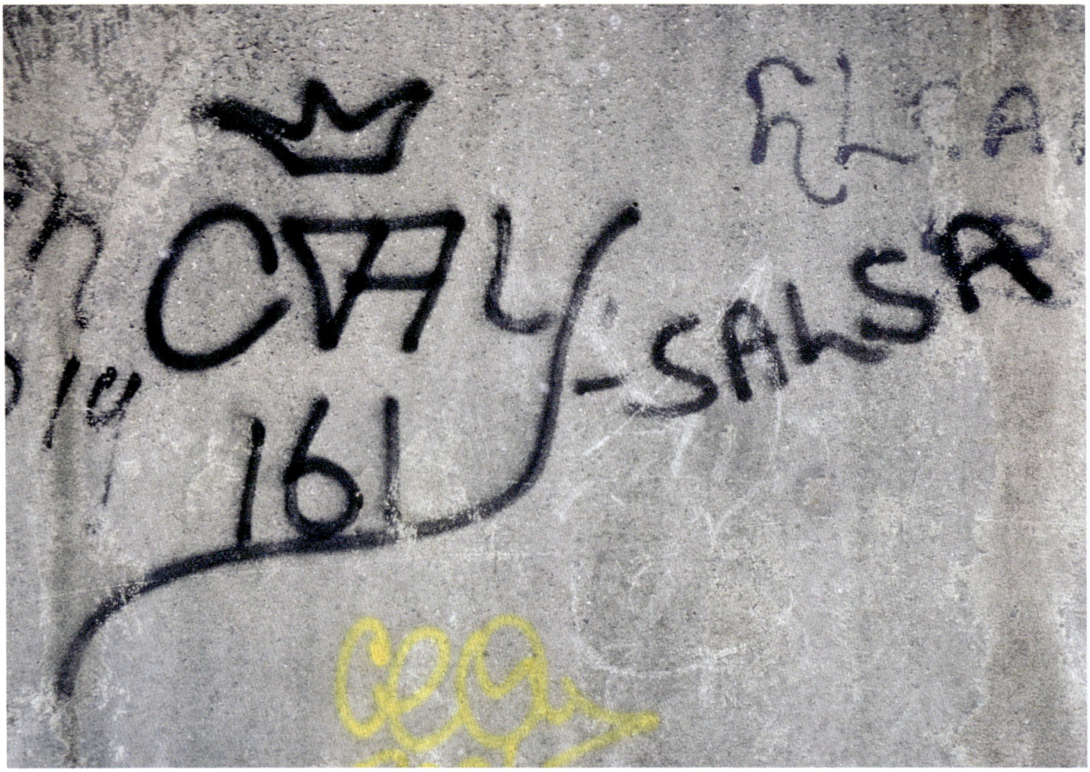

The Name – Street Numbers

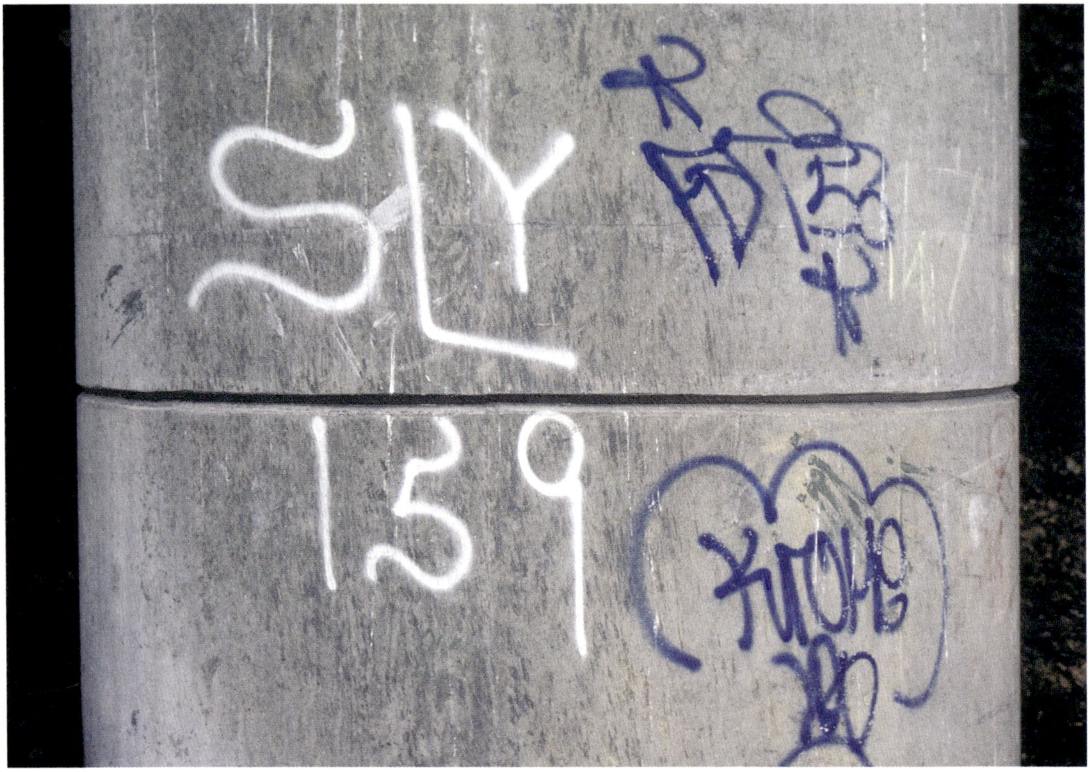

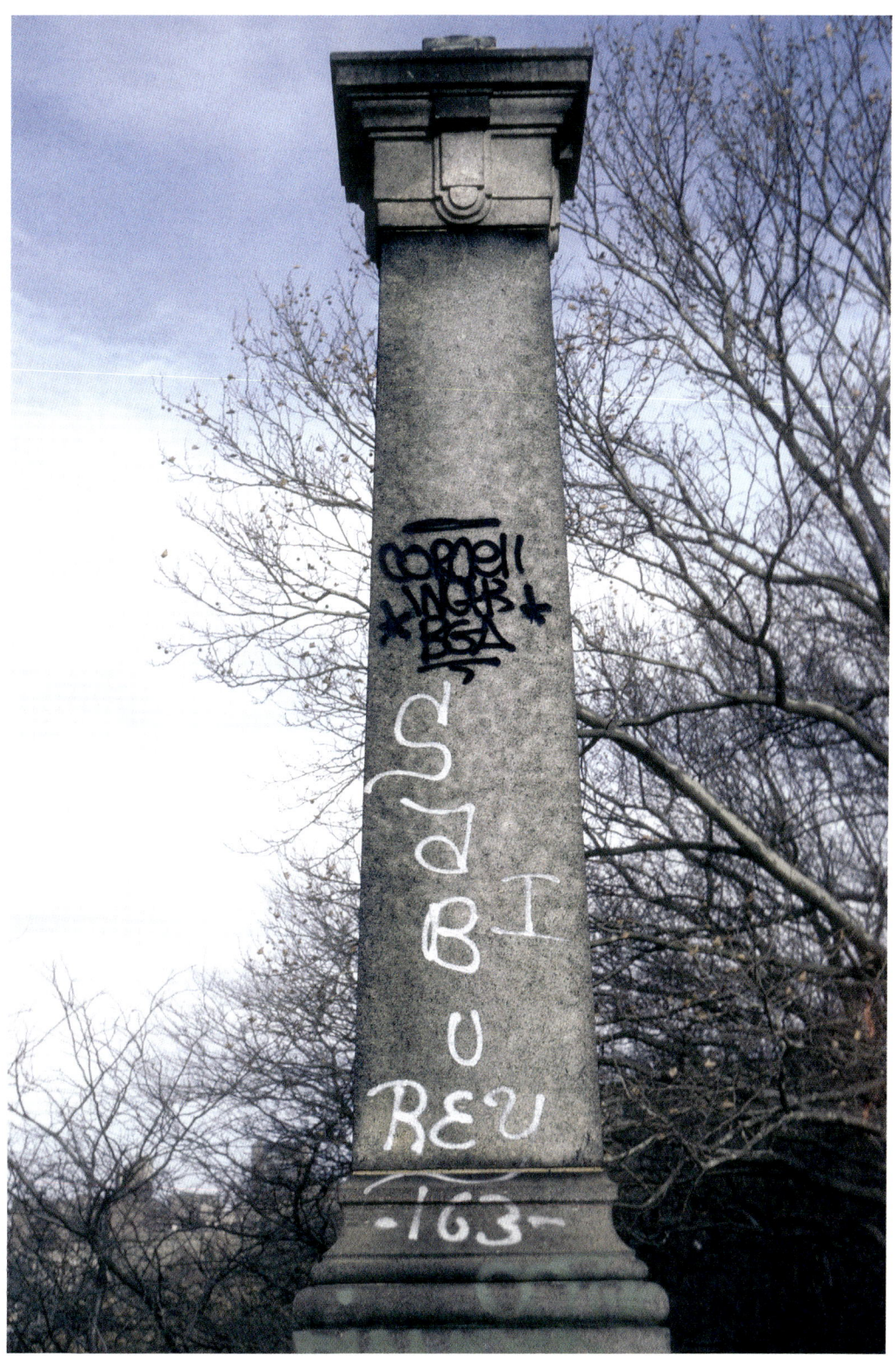

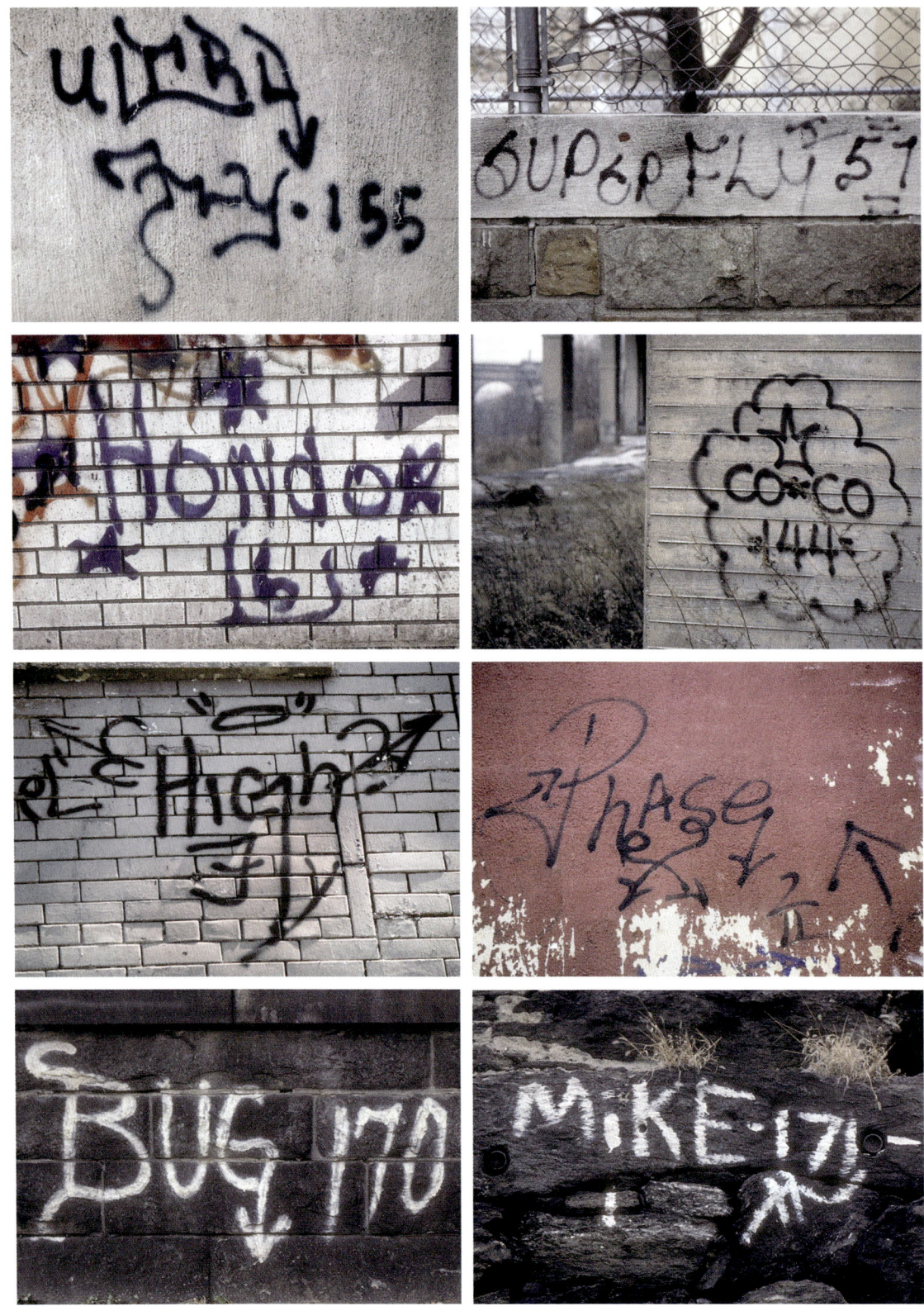

The Name – Street Numbers

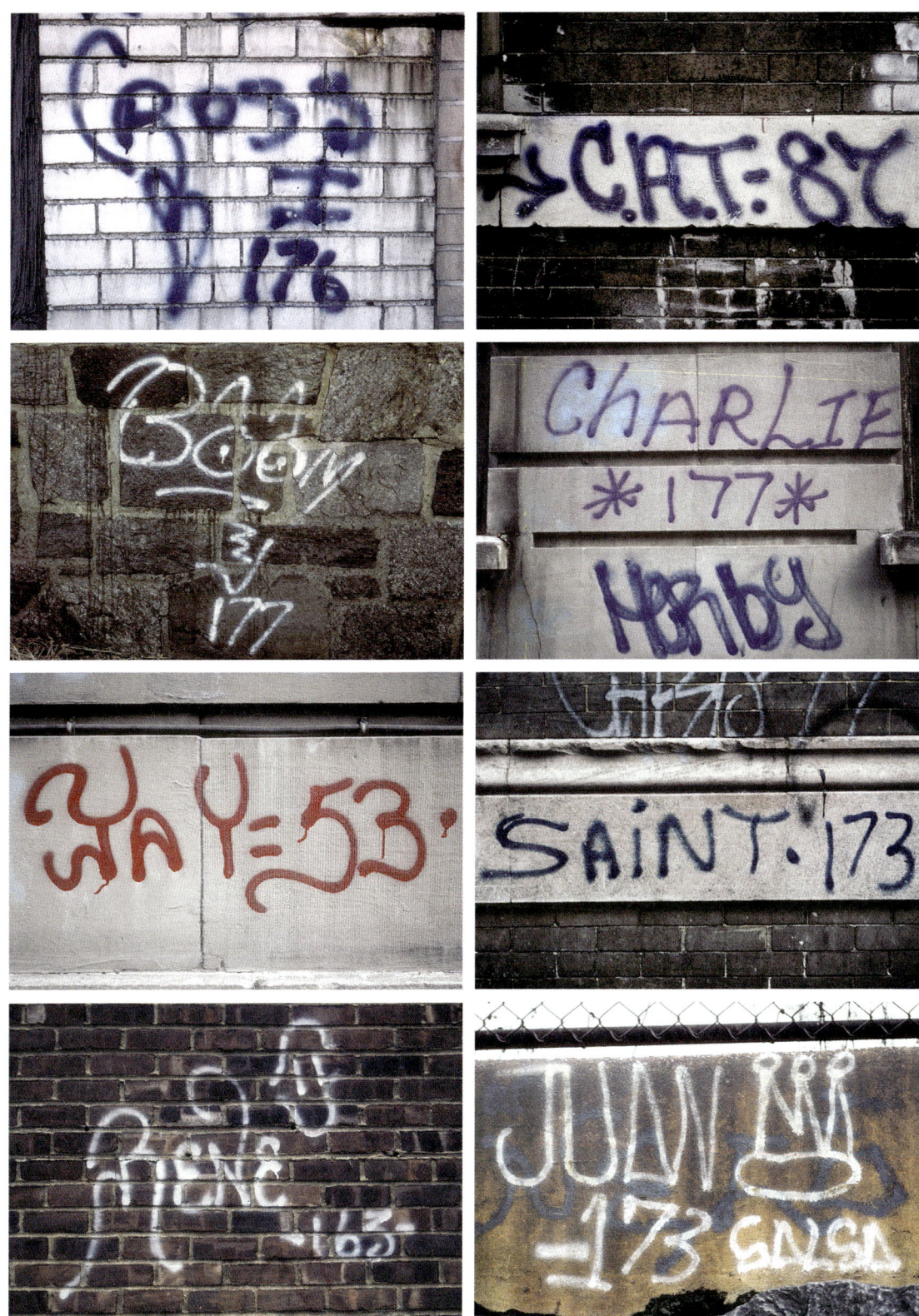

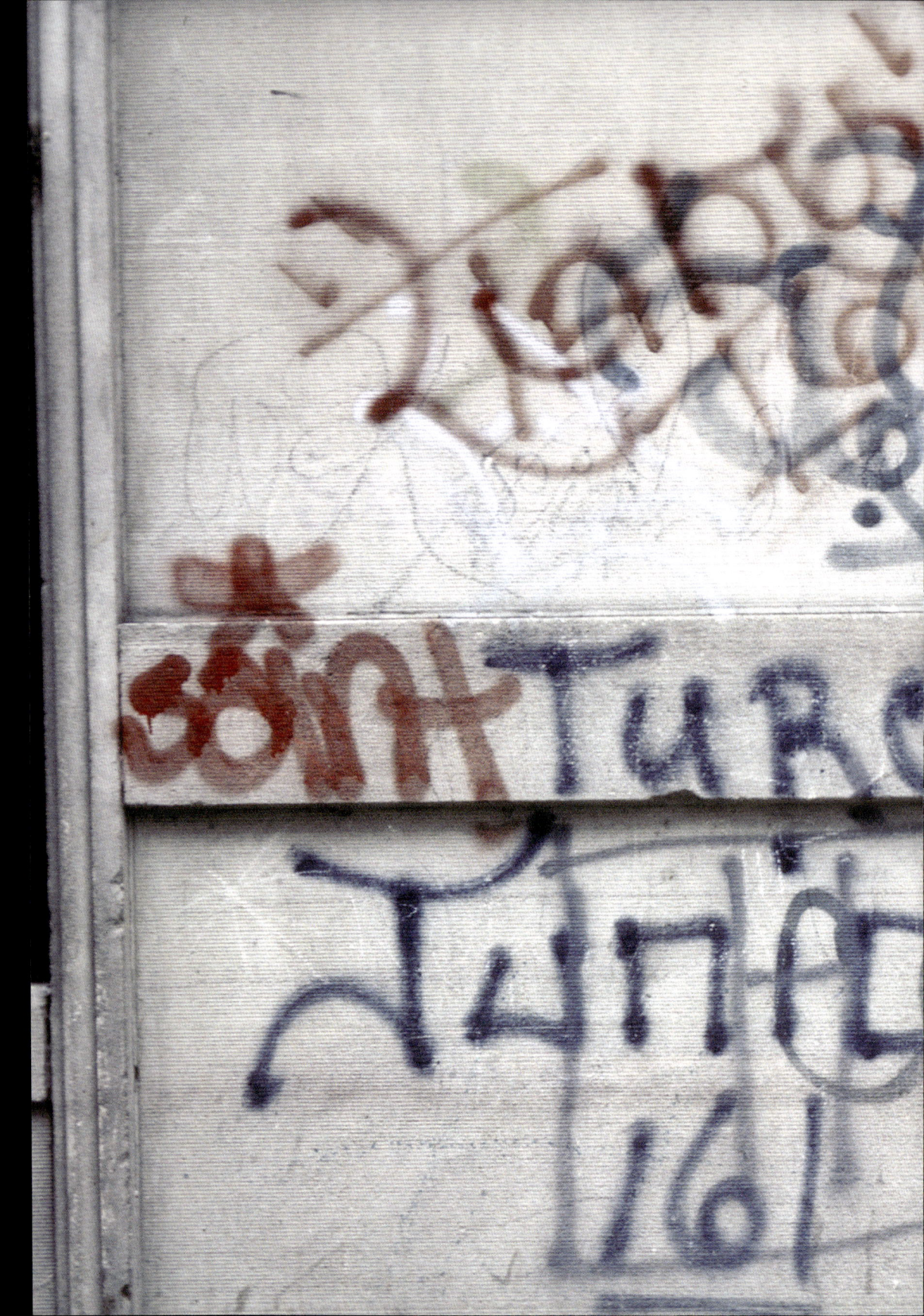

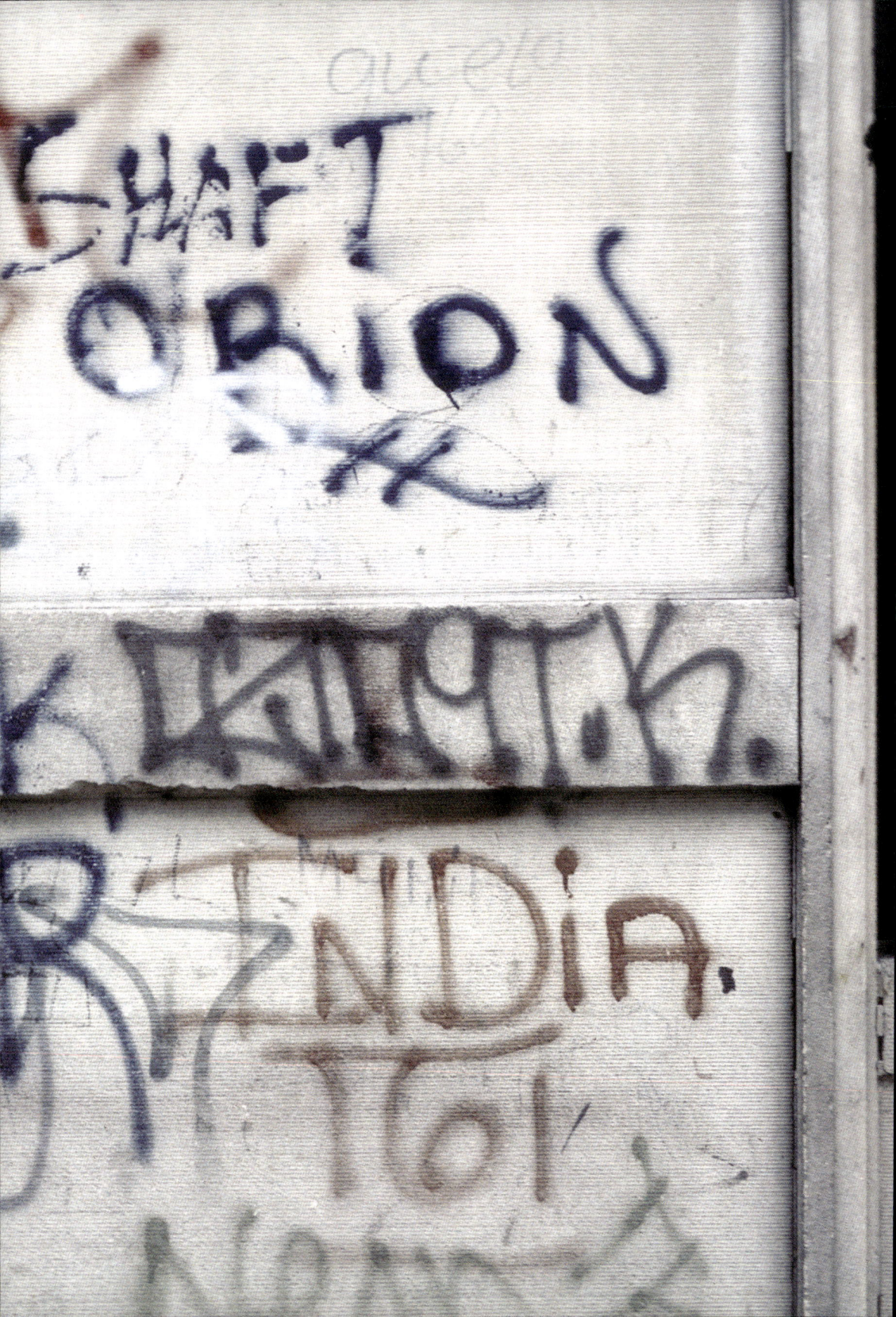

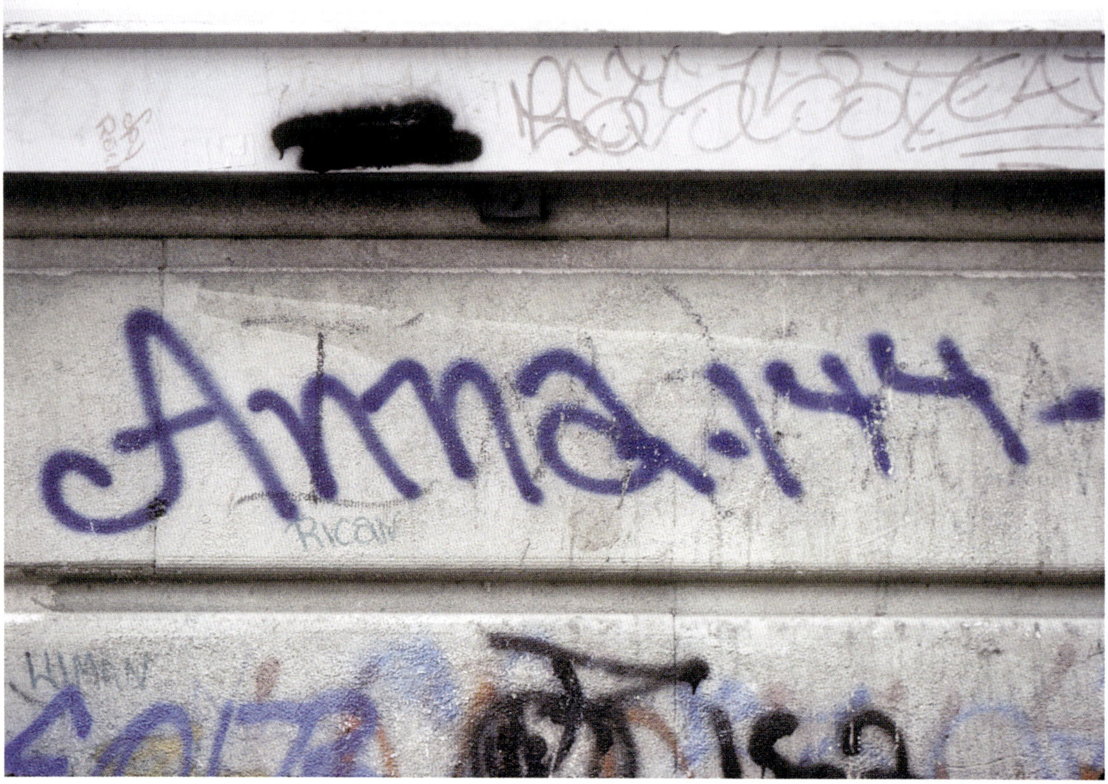

Anna 144

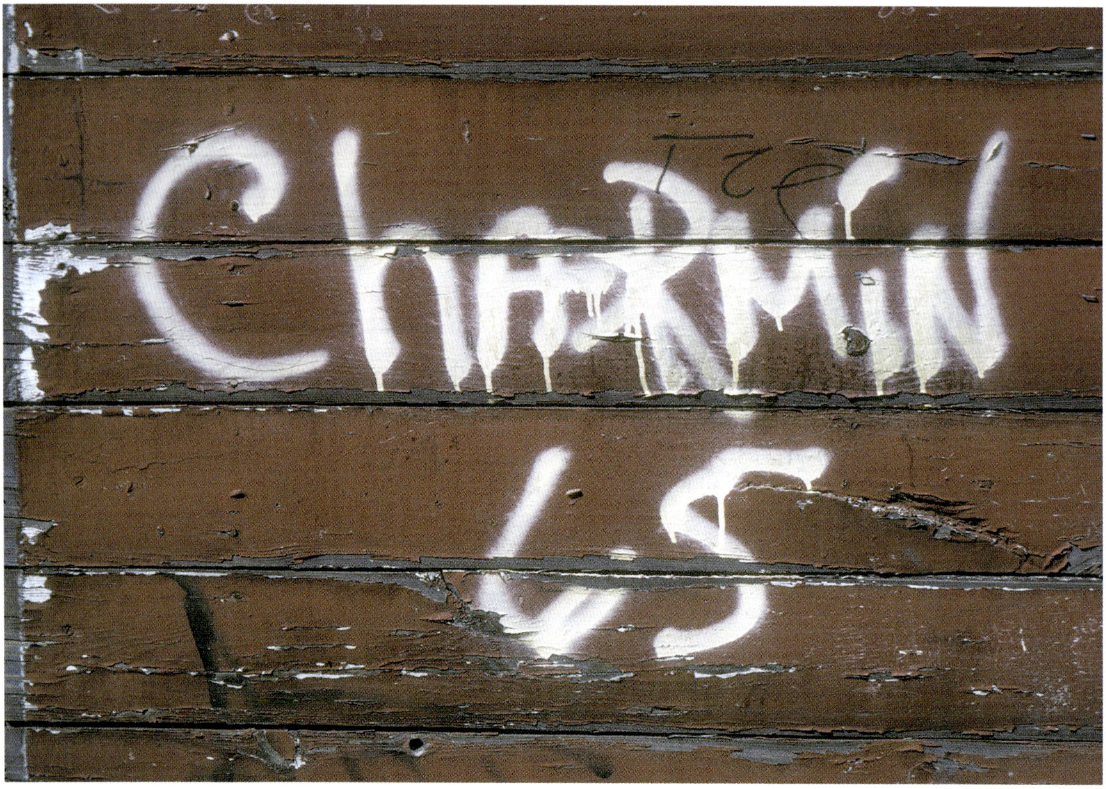

Charmin
65

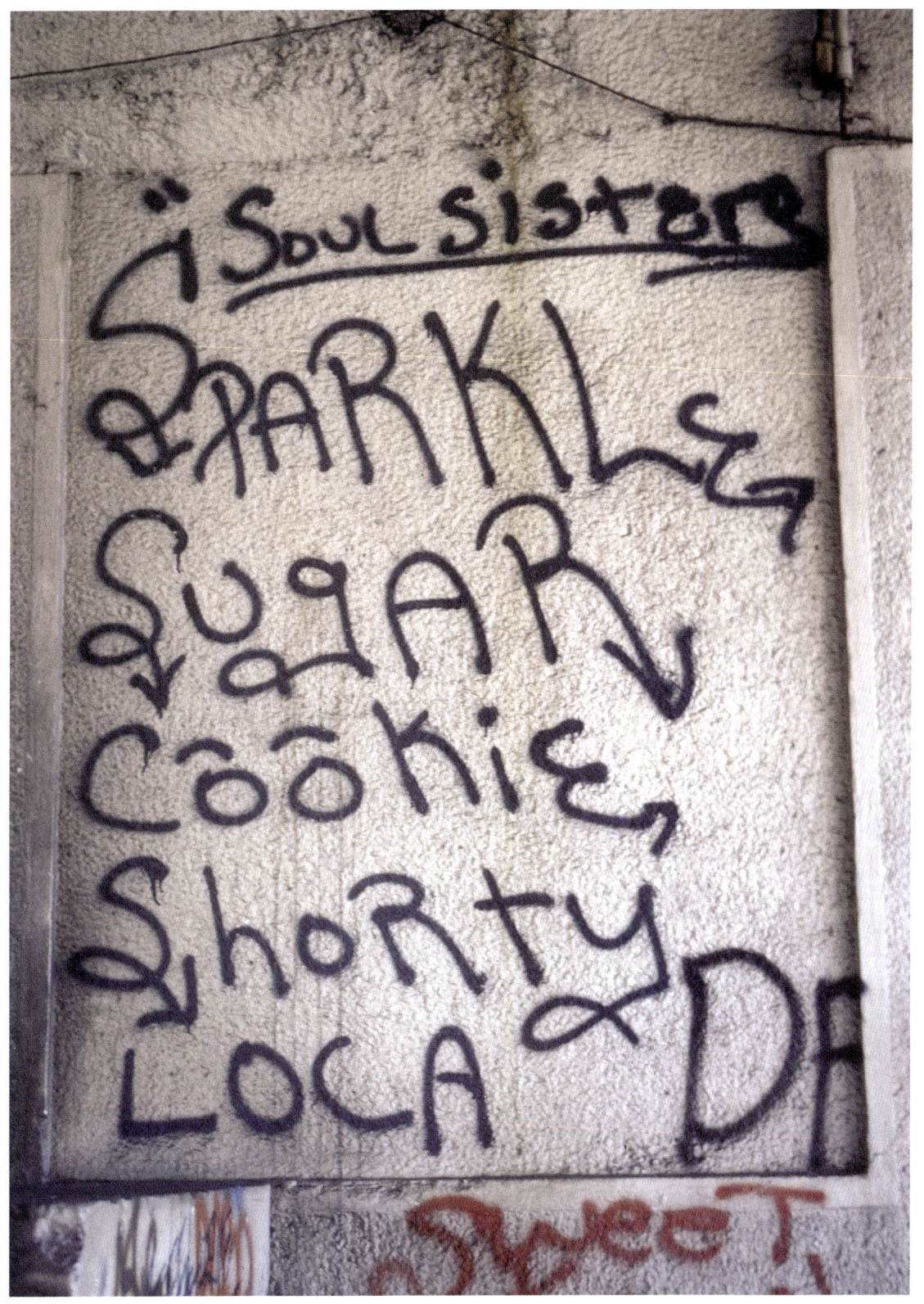

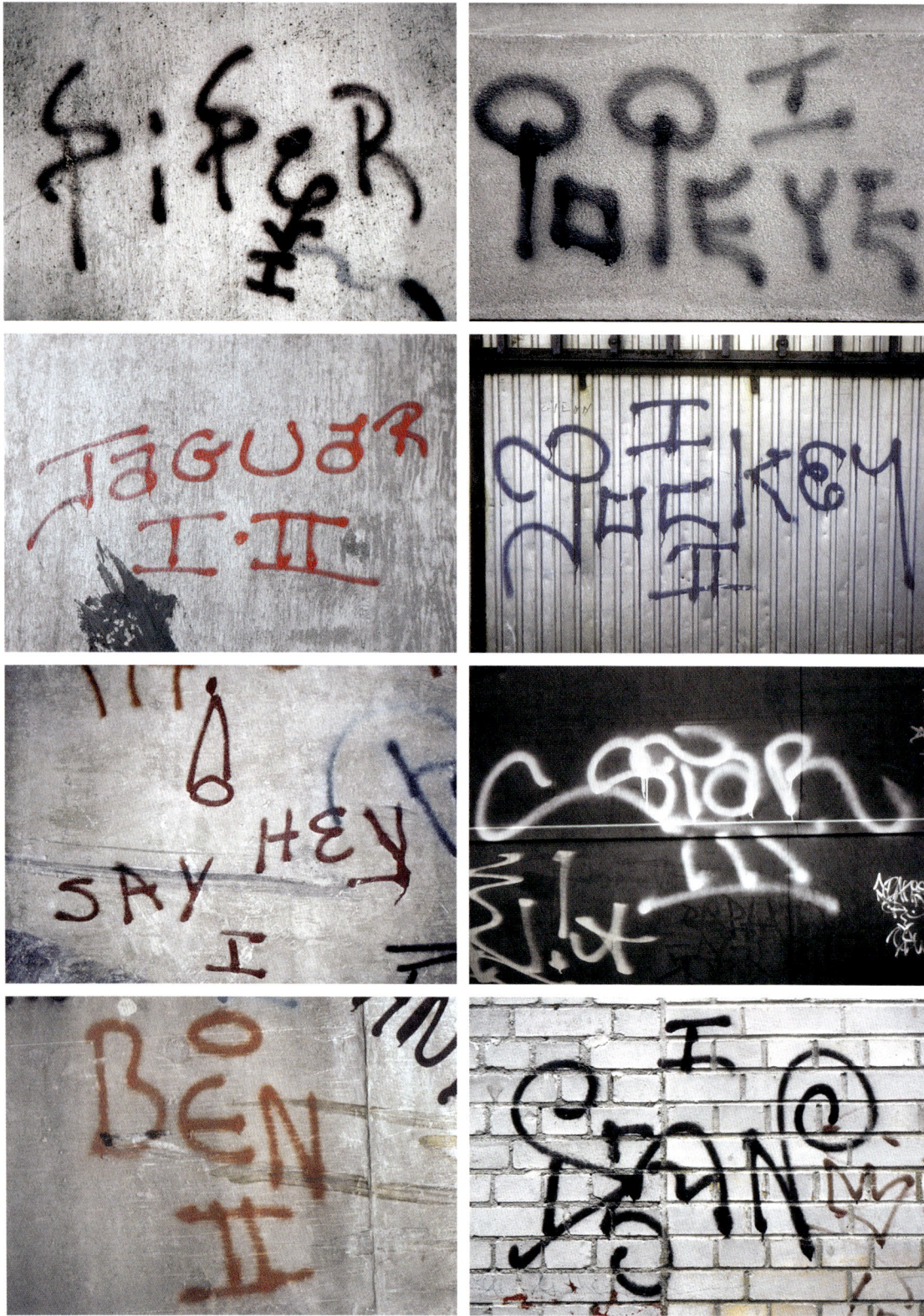

The Name – Roman Numerals

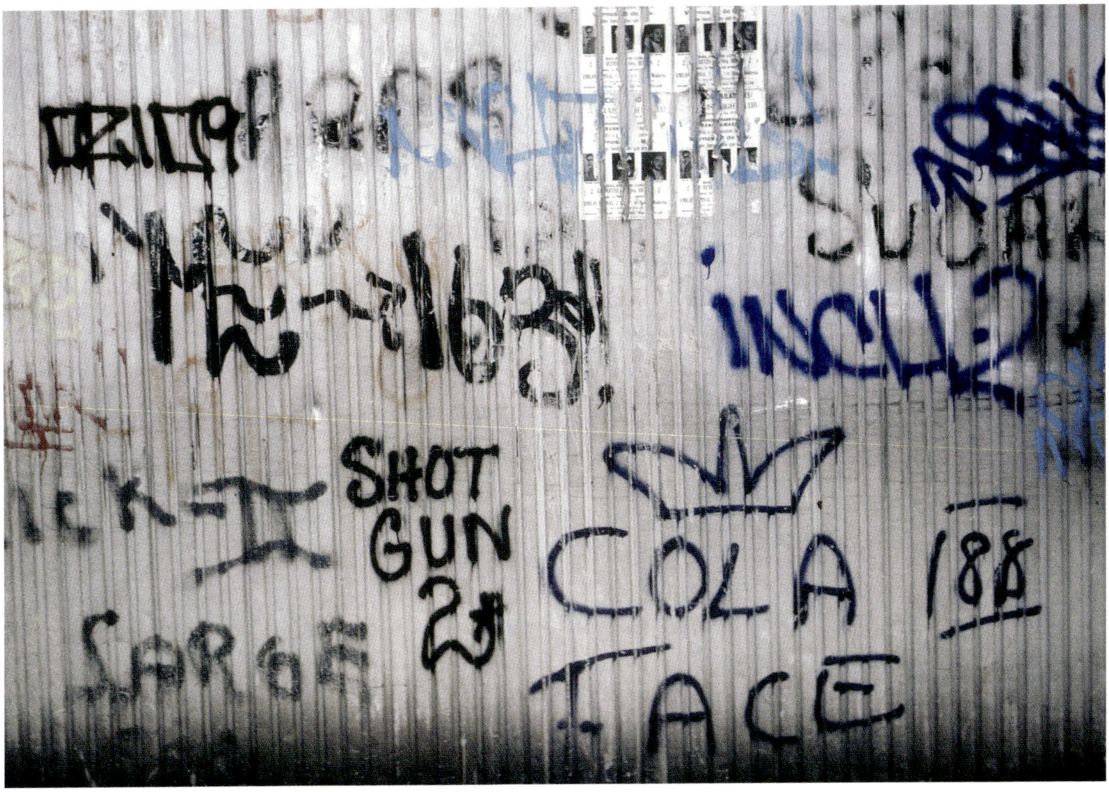

The Name – Roman Numerals

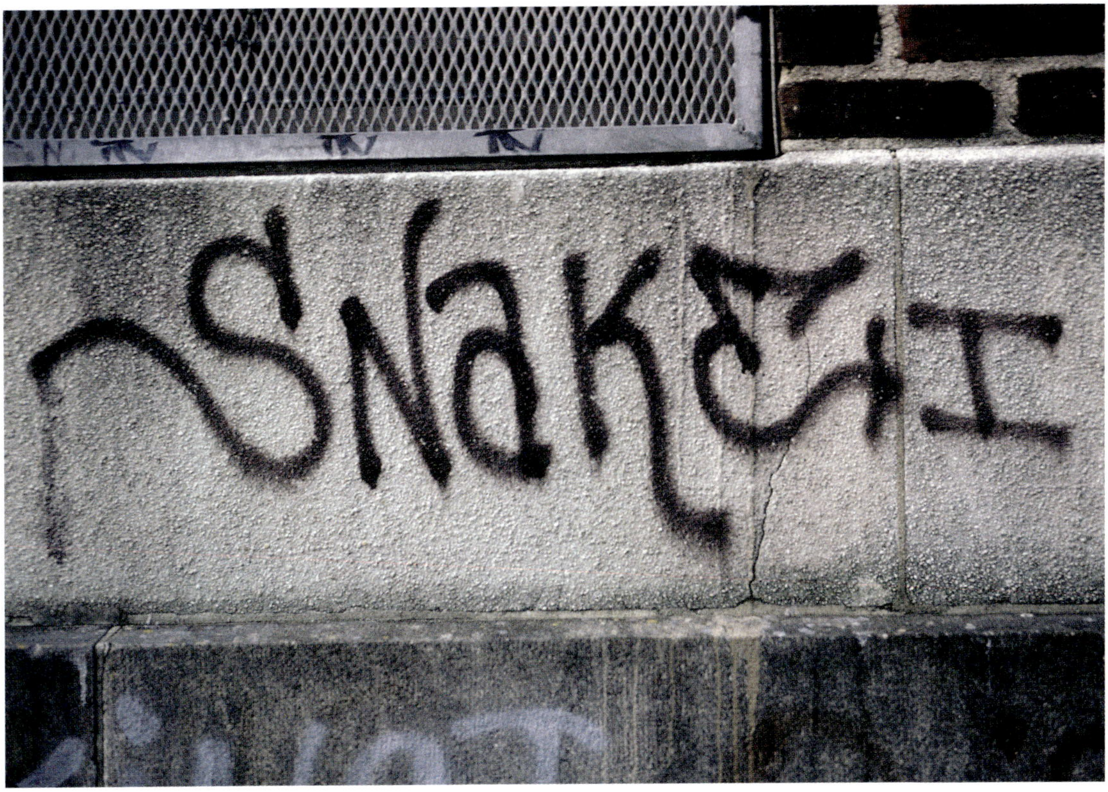

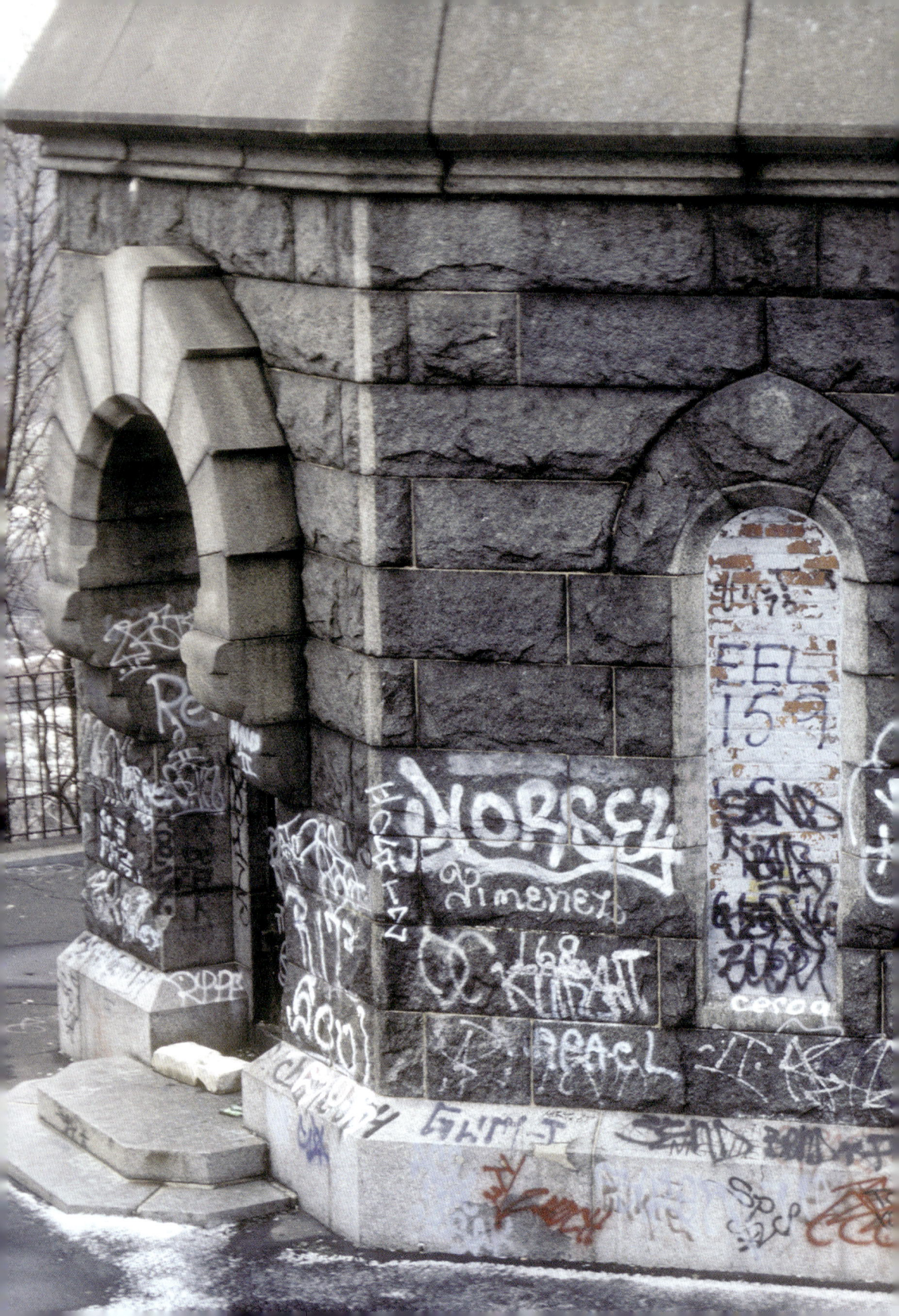

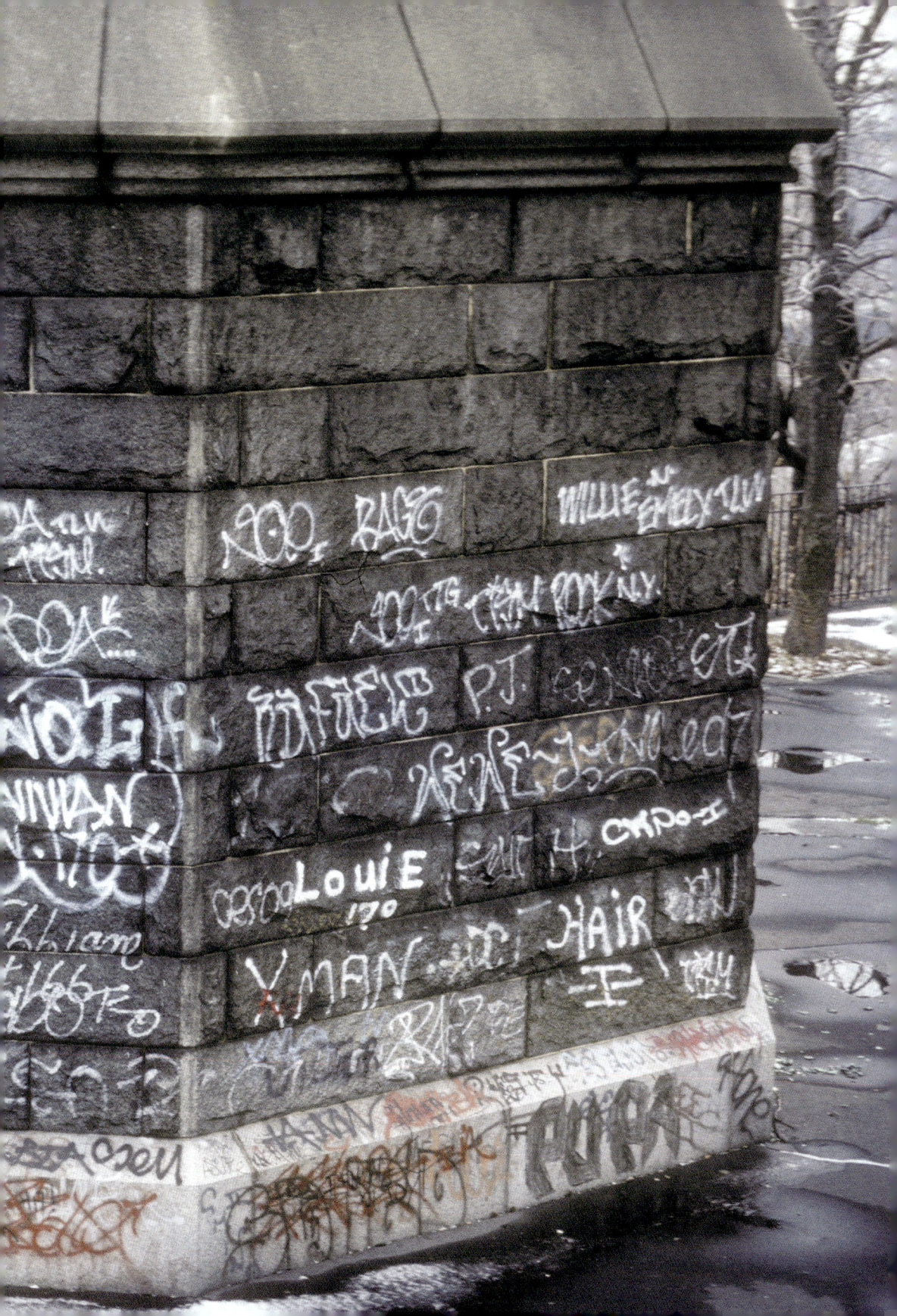

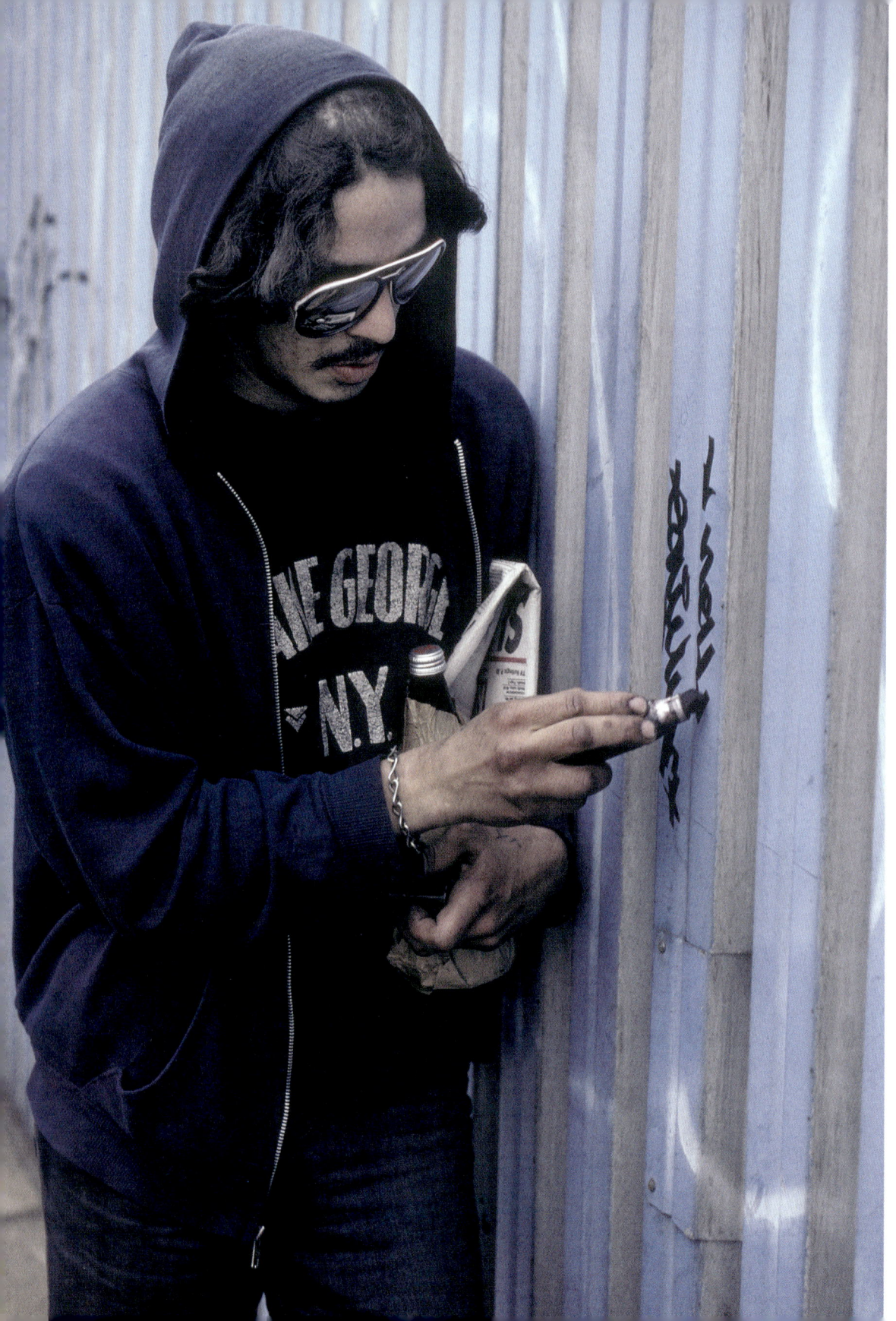

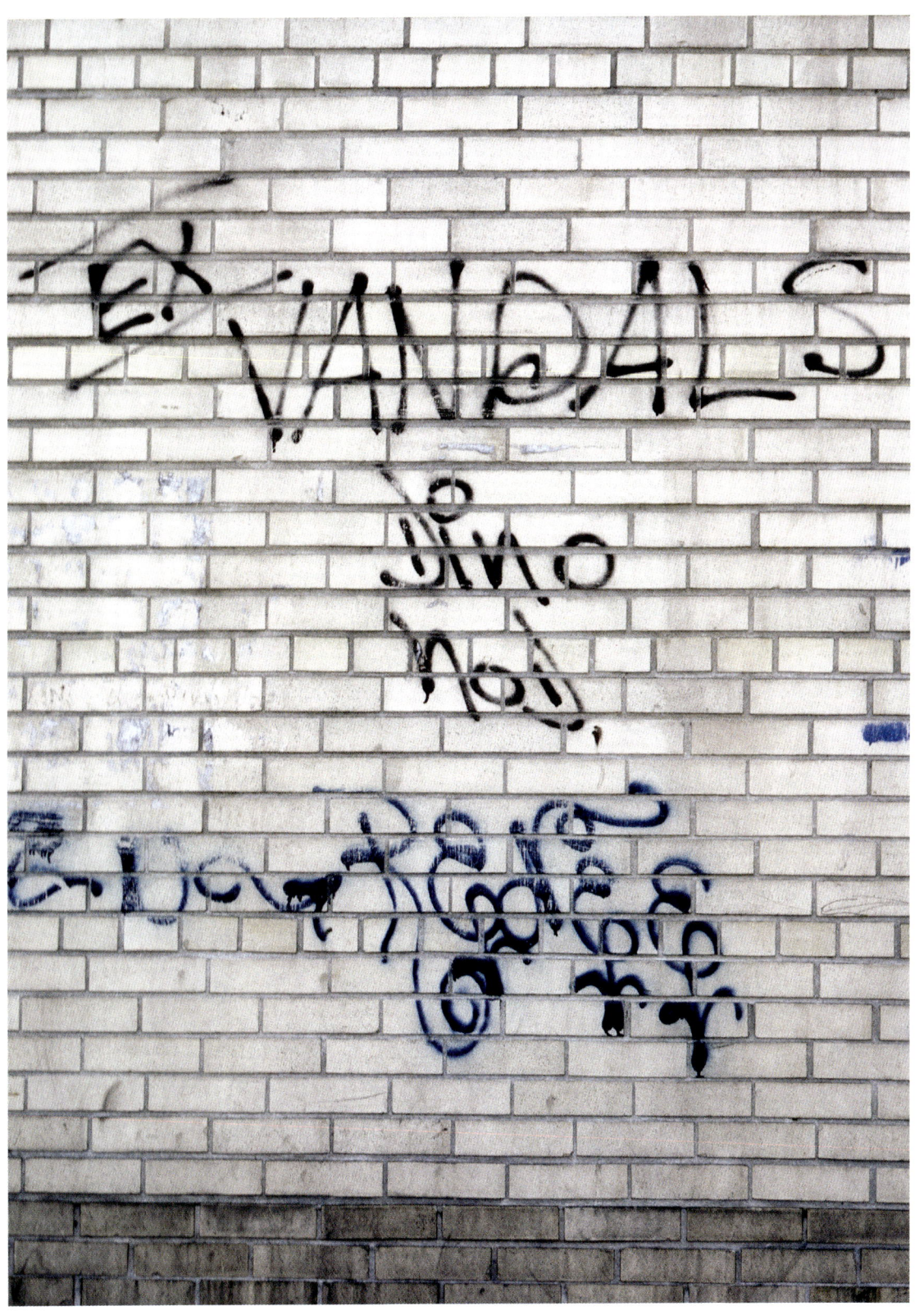

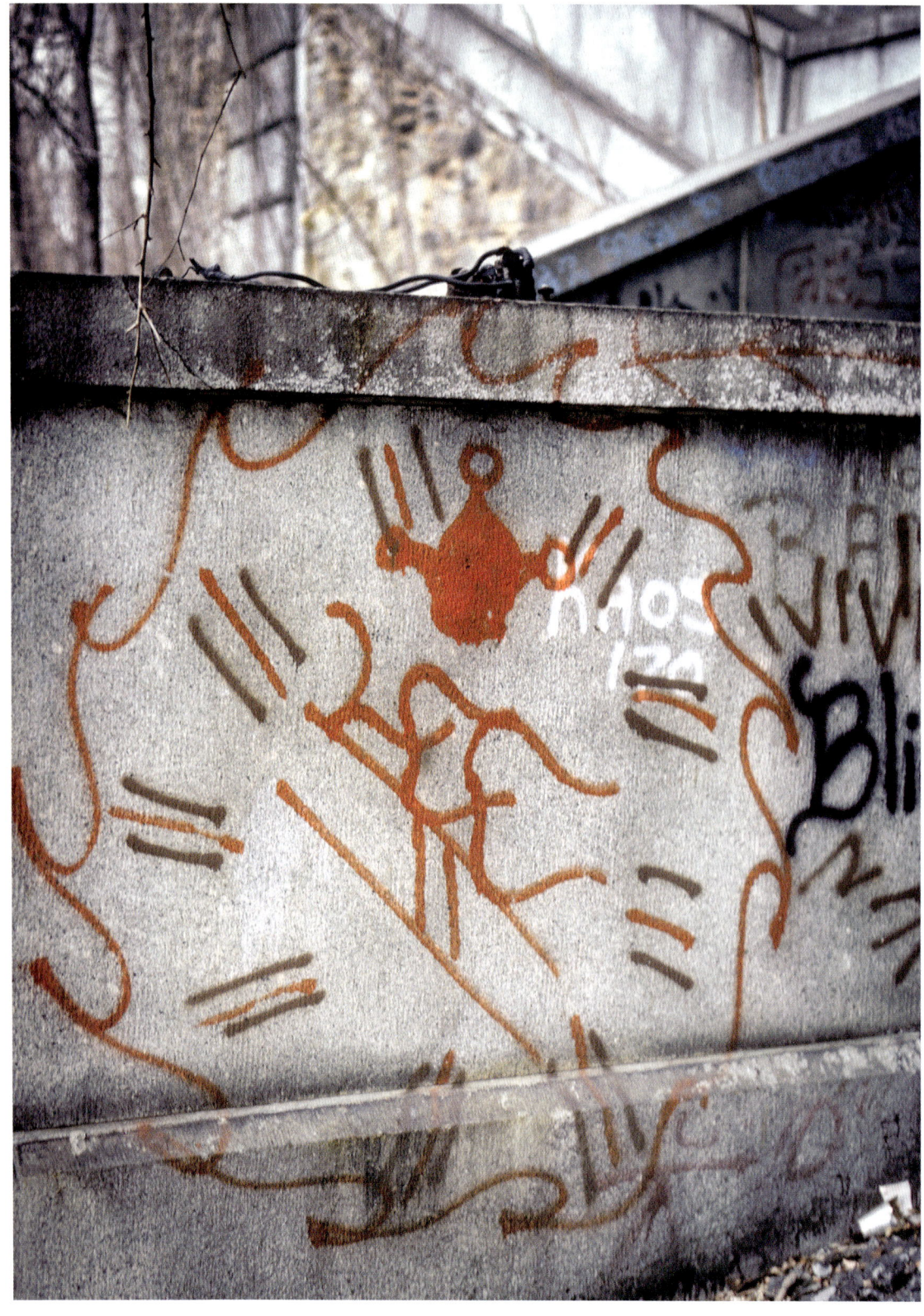

The Name – Variants of the Same Name

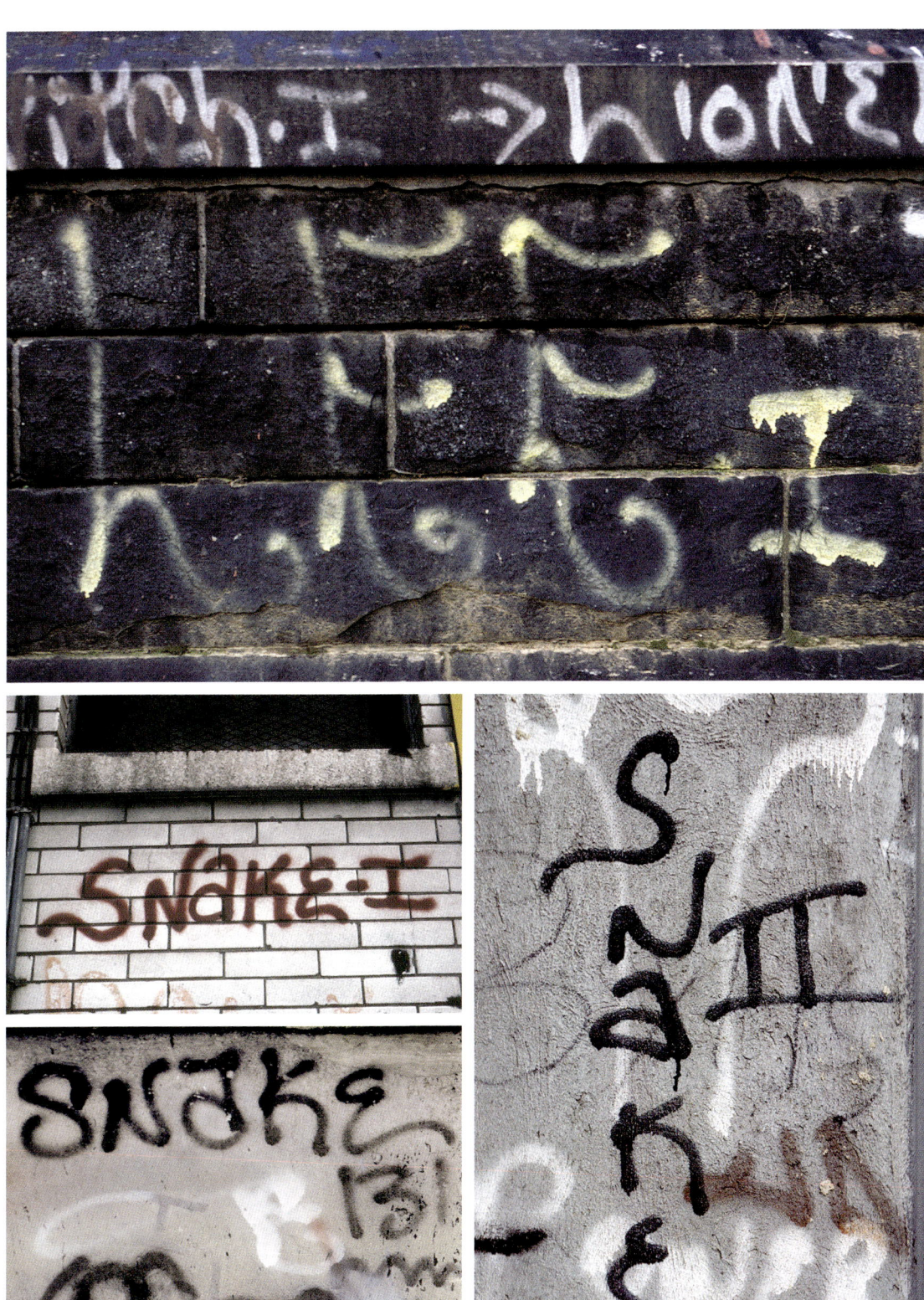

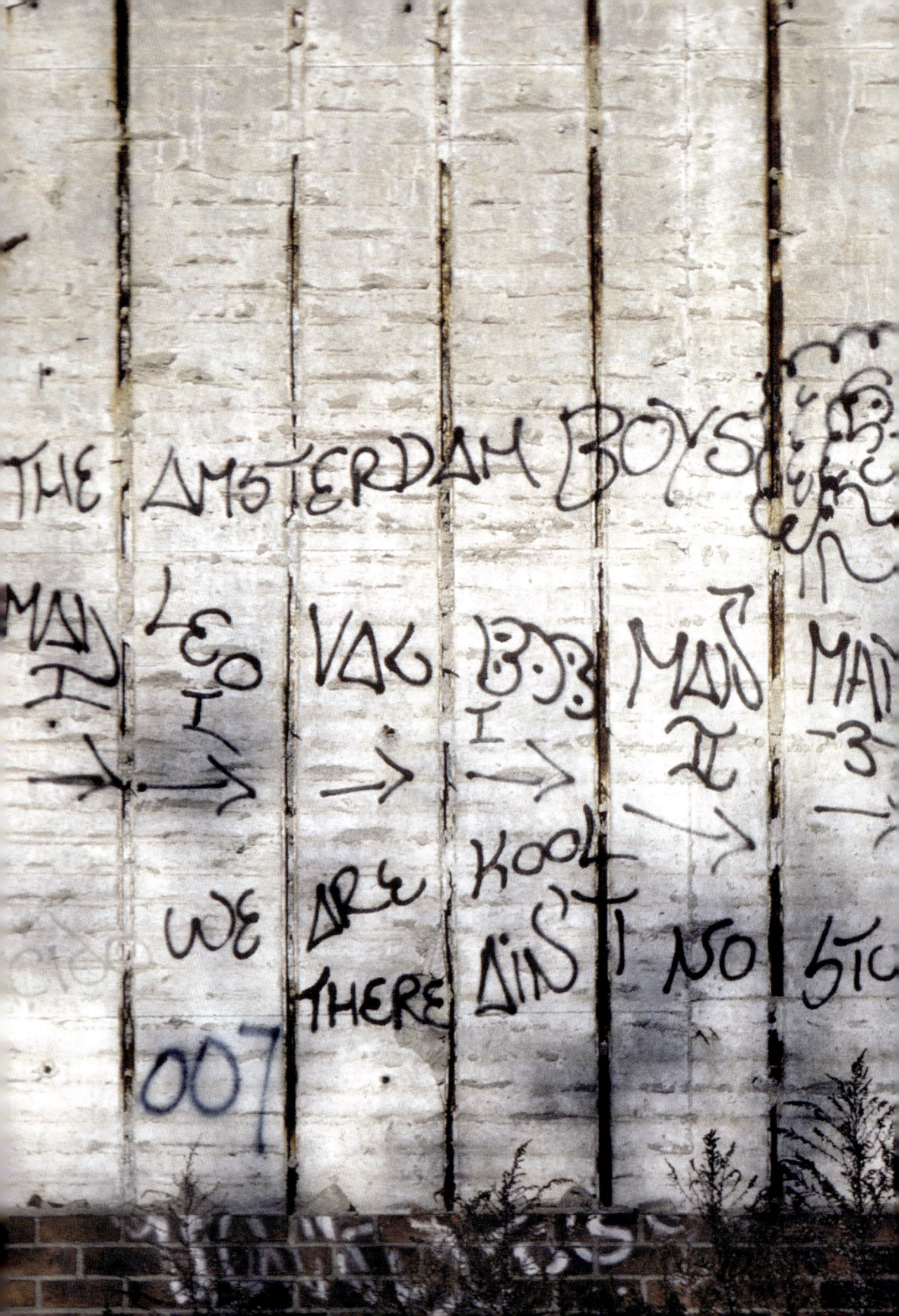

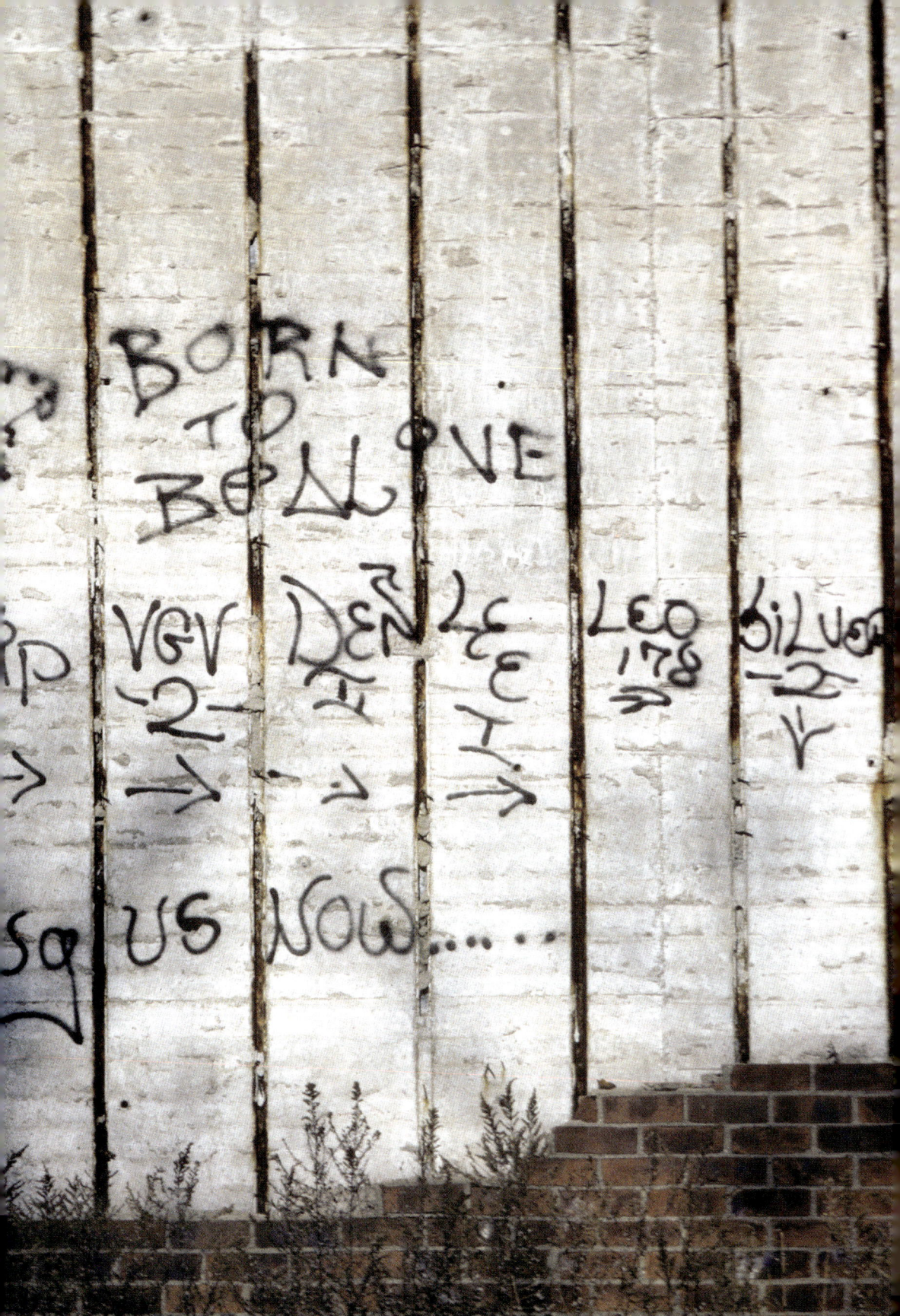

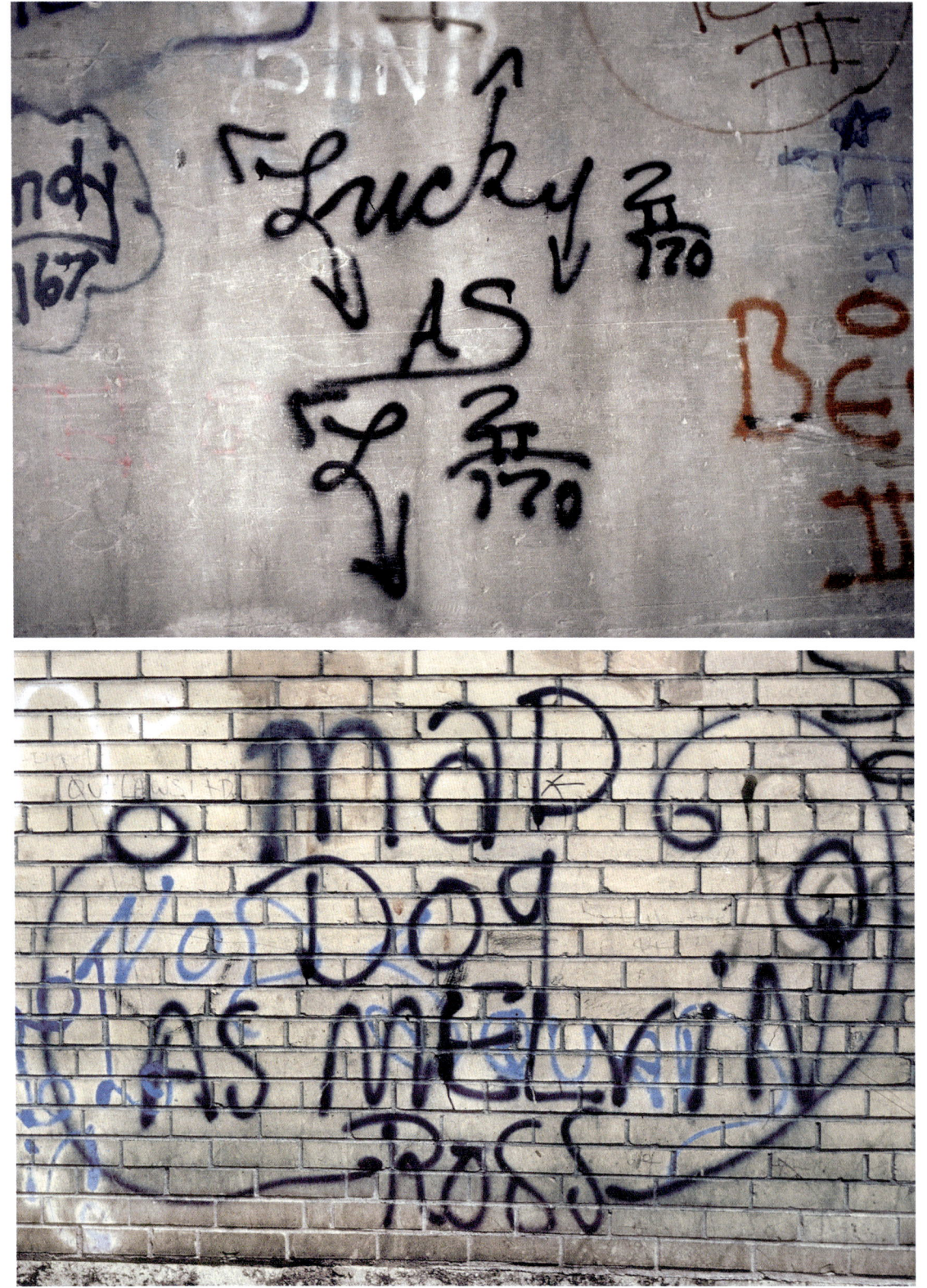

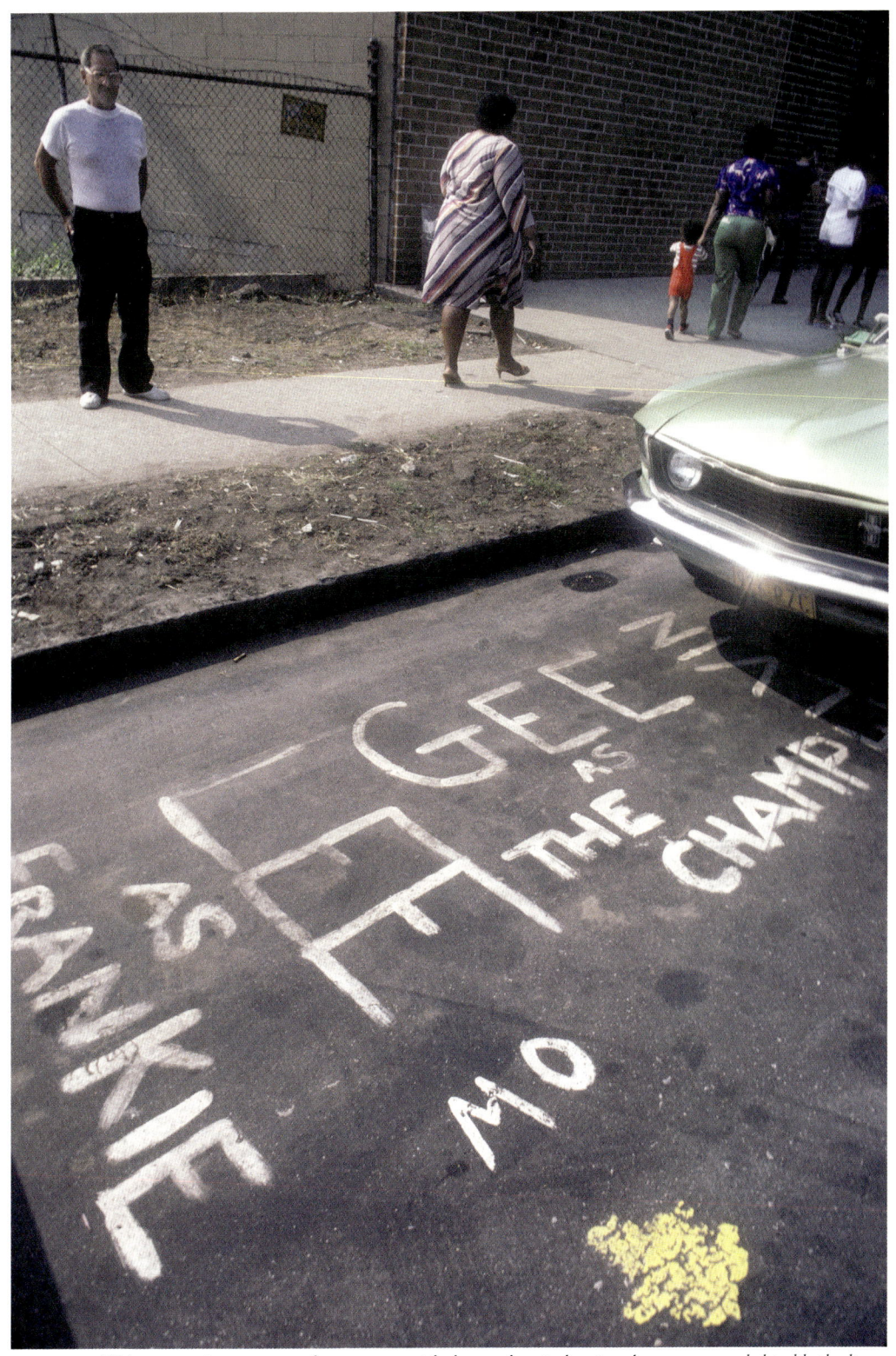

Writers sometimes connected two names with the word as, *indicating the same person behind both aliases.*

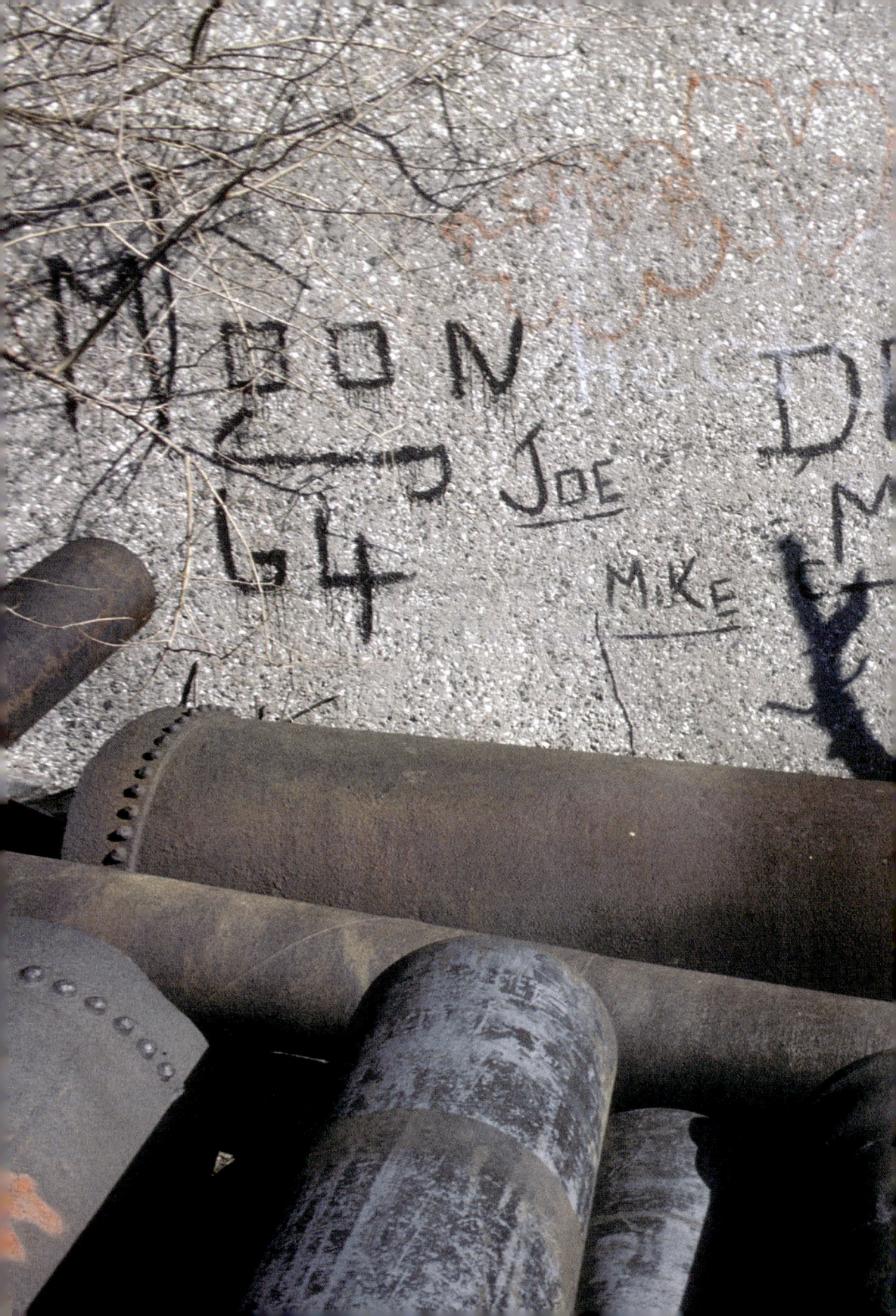

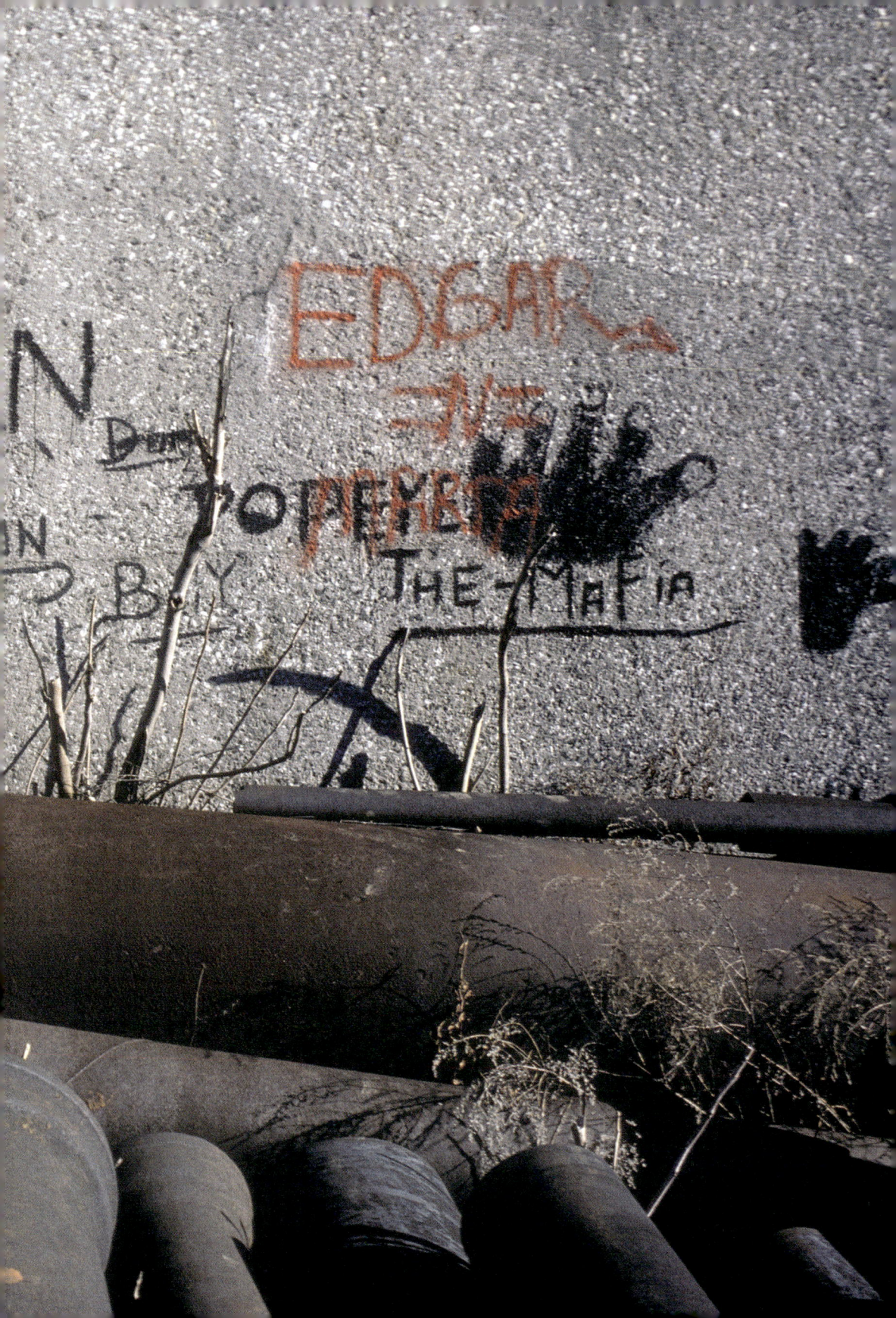

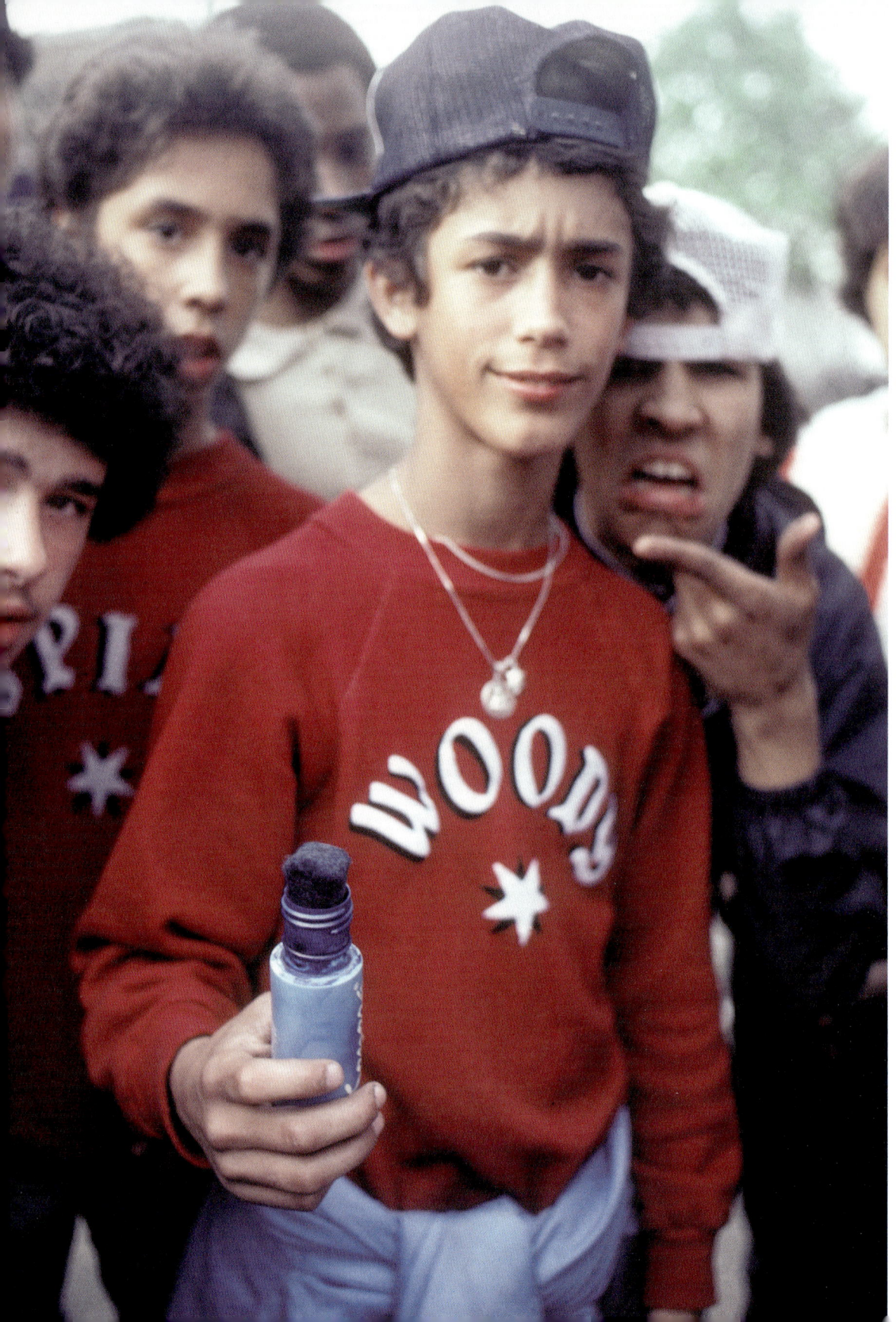

Tools of the Trade

Before the introduction of spray paint and markers, kids wrote their names with whatever they could get their hands on. House paint and brushes were readily available and effective, but unwieldy. The introduction of aerosol paint and permanent markers made the process much easier, and writers quickly adopted these as their tools of choice. By the early 70s, brushes were obsolete.

Writers then, as now, sometimes preferred markers to aerosol because pens are easier to carry, make no sound when used, and dry quickly. Markers write most smoothly and adhere best on surfaces such as tile, glass and metal. Ink, however, is less permanent than spray paint. Kids generally used black markers with wide tips for hitting walls but kept an array of colors, gleaned from art stores, for designing pieces in their sketch books.

Some writers resorted to "inventing" markers from hardware shops they traveled out of their neighborhoods to patronize. Others crafted their own. One method was to empty the fluid from a Zippo ciga-rette lighter case, fill it with Flowmaster ink, stuff cotton or felt from a blackboard eraser into the cavity and then trim the edge.

Blade made specialized markers from Absorbine Jr. This remedy for aches and pains came in bottles with foam applicators. He filled these with white shoe polish and hit windows on the number 1 and 3 trains. But the foam tip, meant for spreading balm on skin, was too delicate to write on anything other than windows.

Spray paint is difficult to control, and writers worked long and hard to devise and master the techniques of their new medium. At first the only colors available were black, white, blue and red, but kids soon learned where to find every color and brand manufactured. They also discovered that nozzles with wide and thin jets could be interchanged. The wider spray enabled them to cover large, rough surfaces quickly and smoothly as they could move their arm freely. With practice, they developed the expertise to paint more elegant and sophisticated tags and pieces.

Woody showing his choice of marker. Doze is posing to the right.

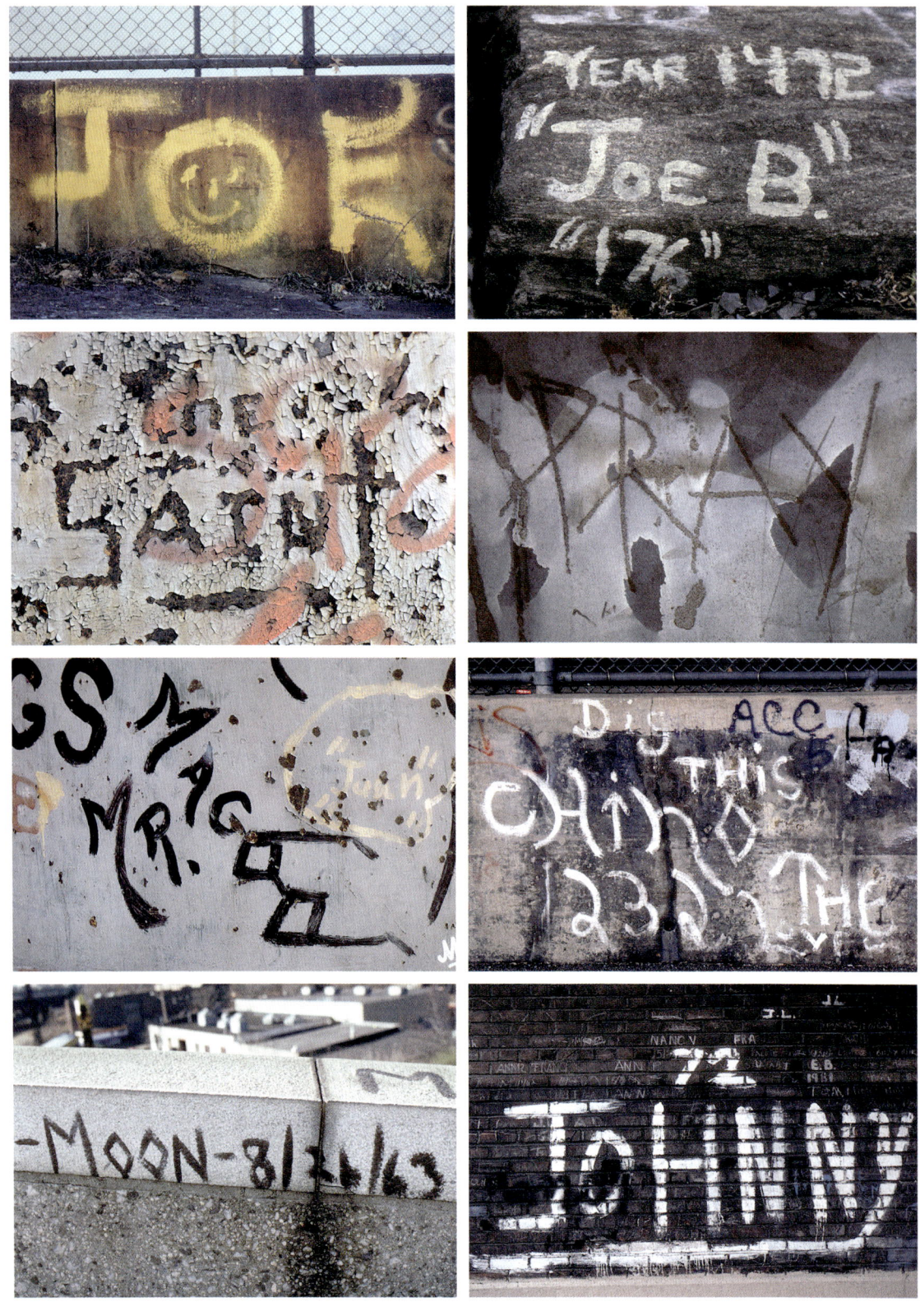

Tools of the Trade – Brush and Scratch

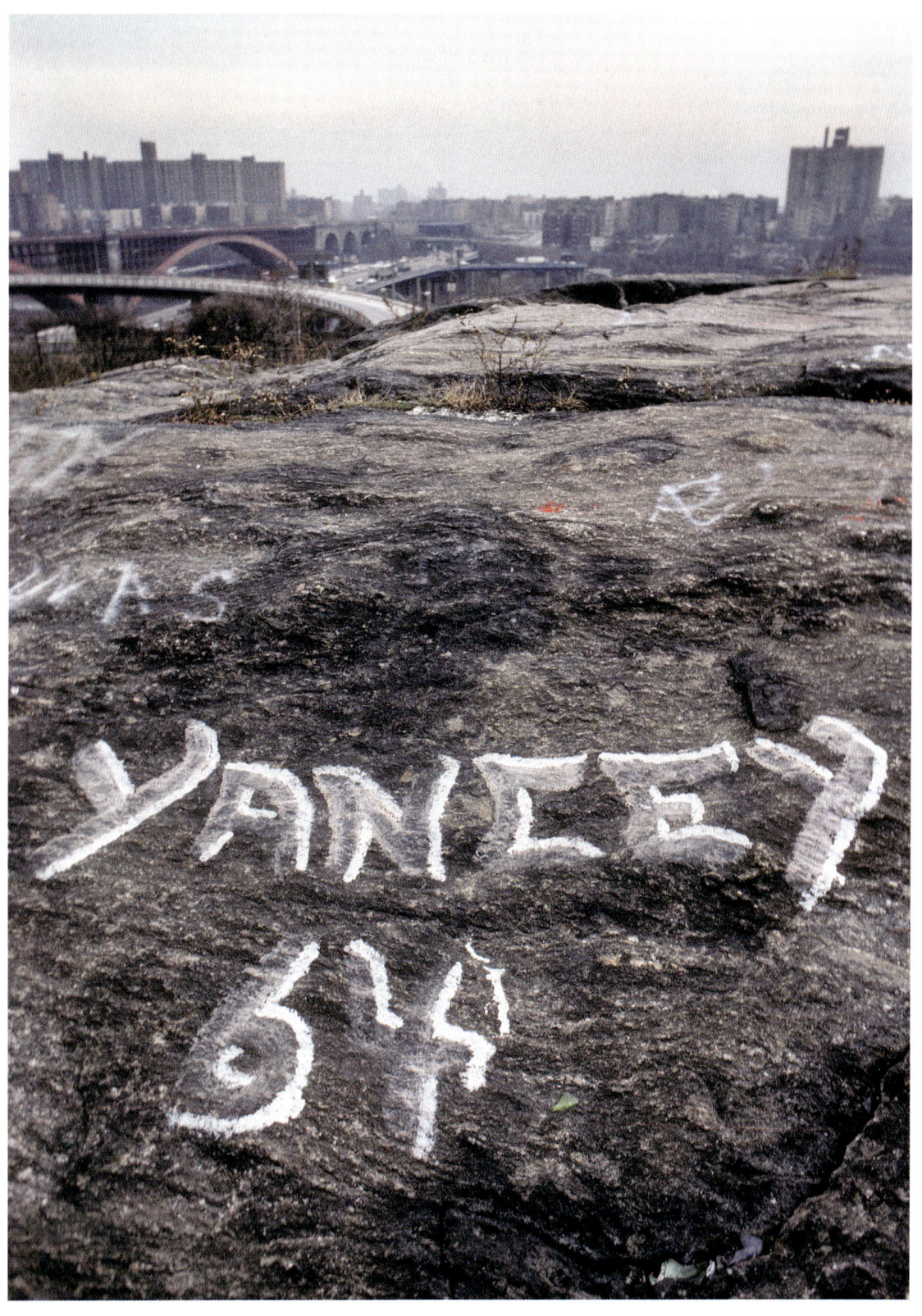

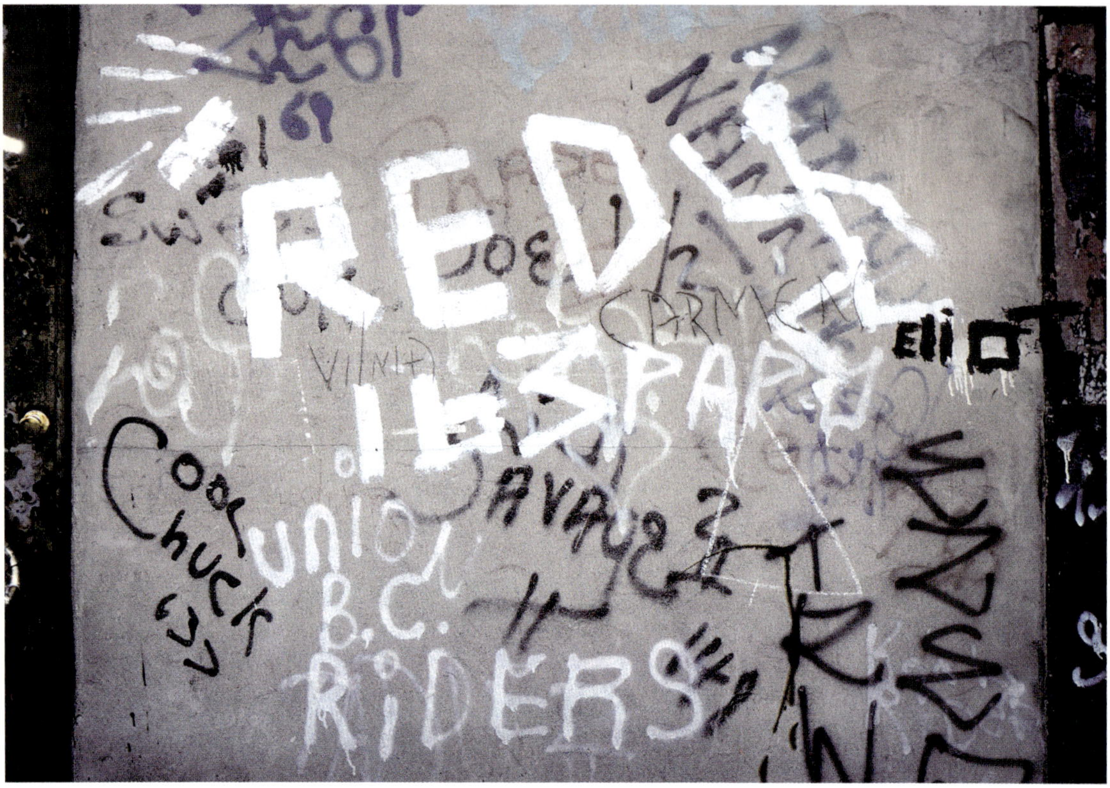

Tools of the Trade – Brush

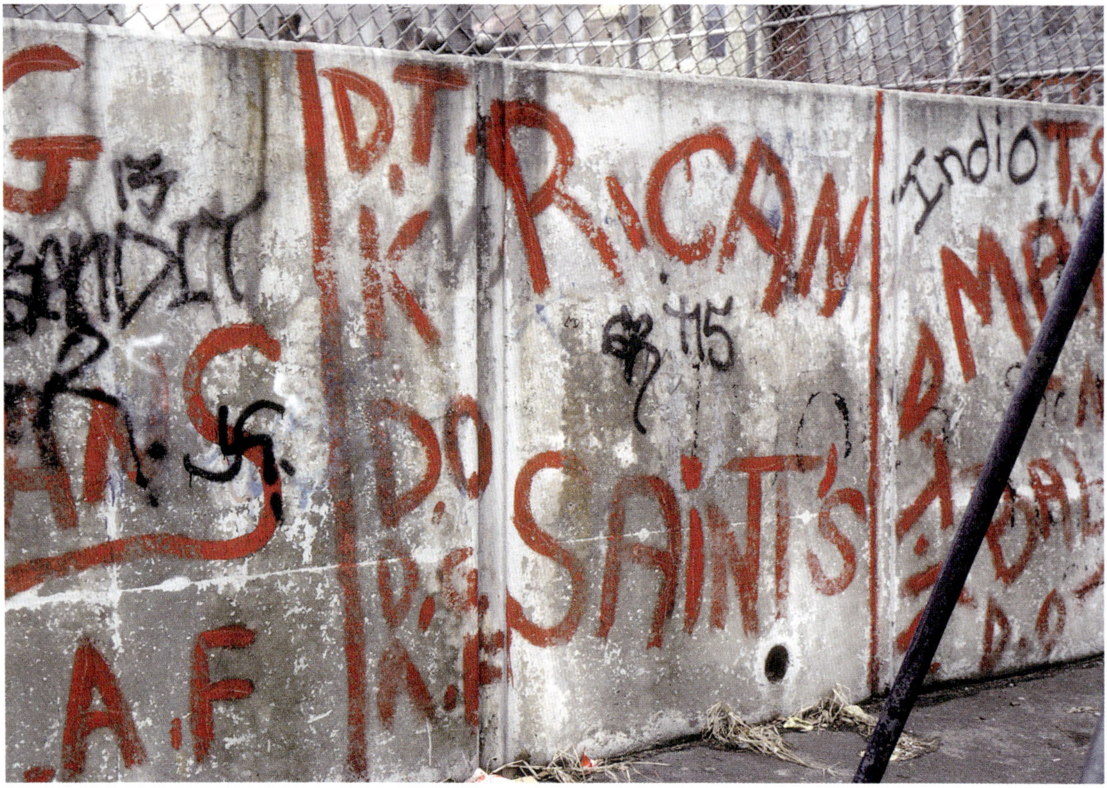

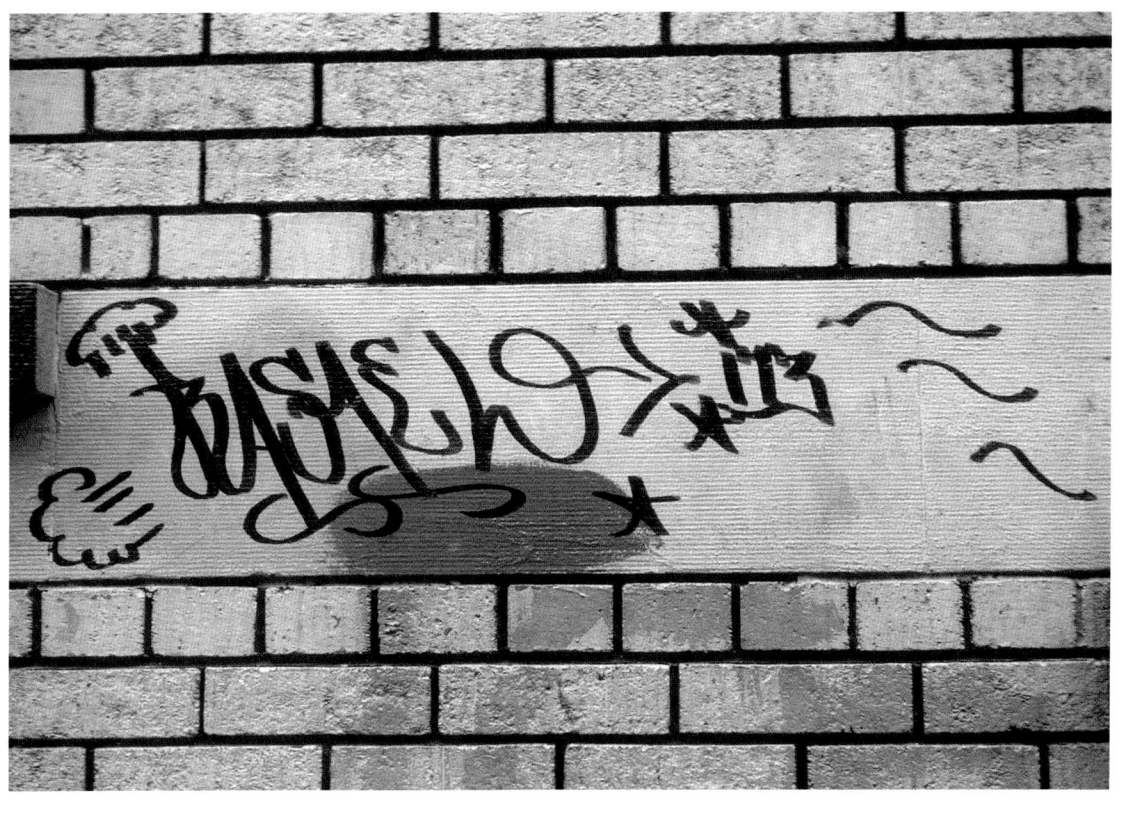

Overleaf: Frosty Freeze from Rock Steady Crew.

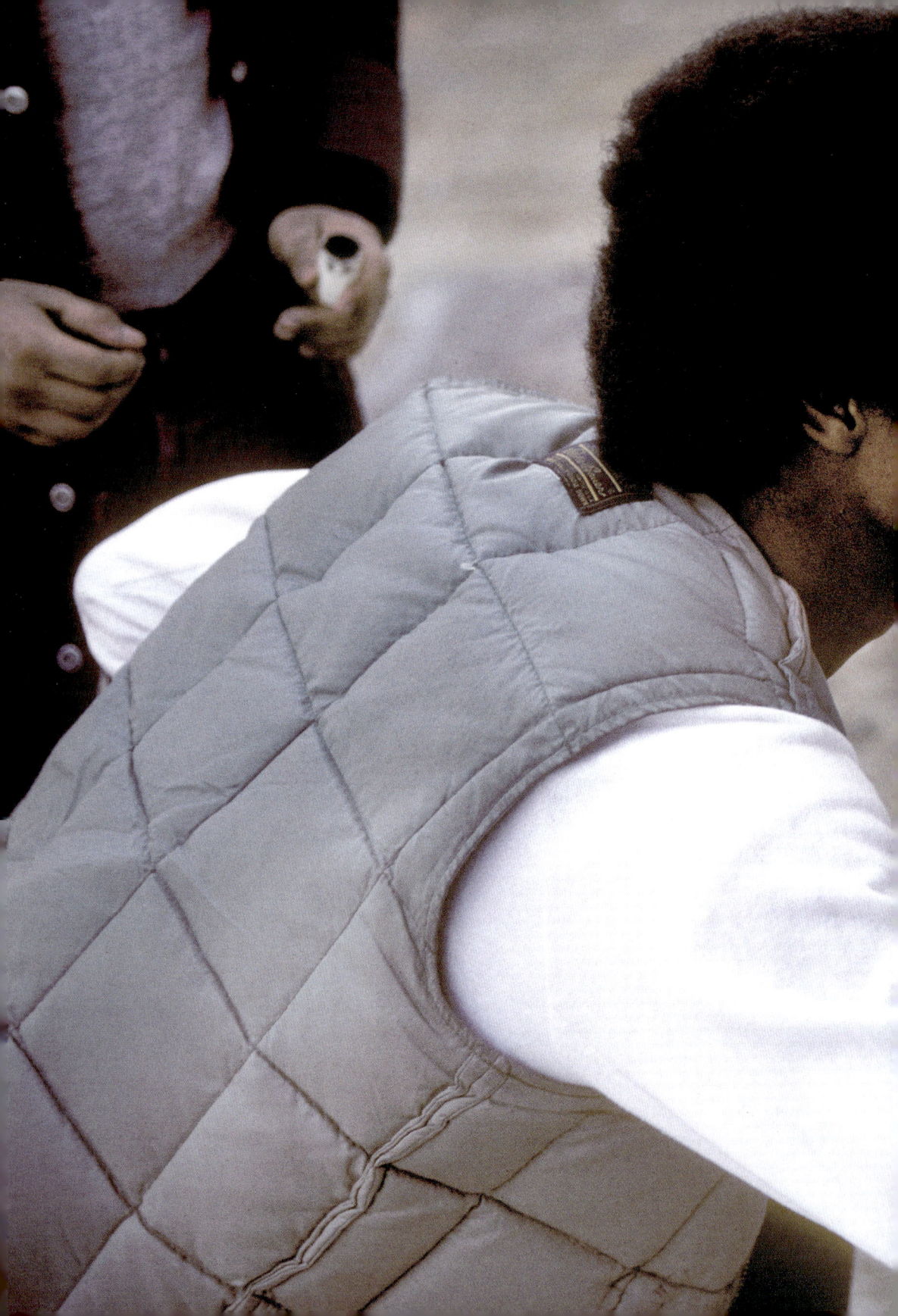

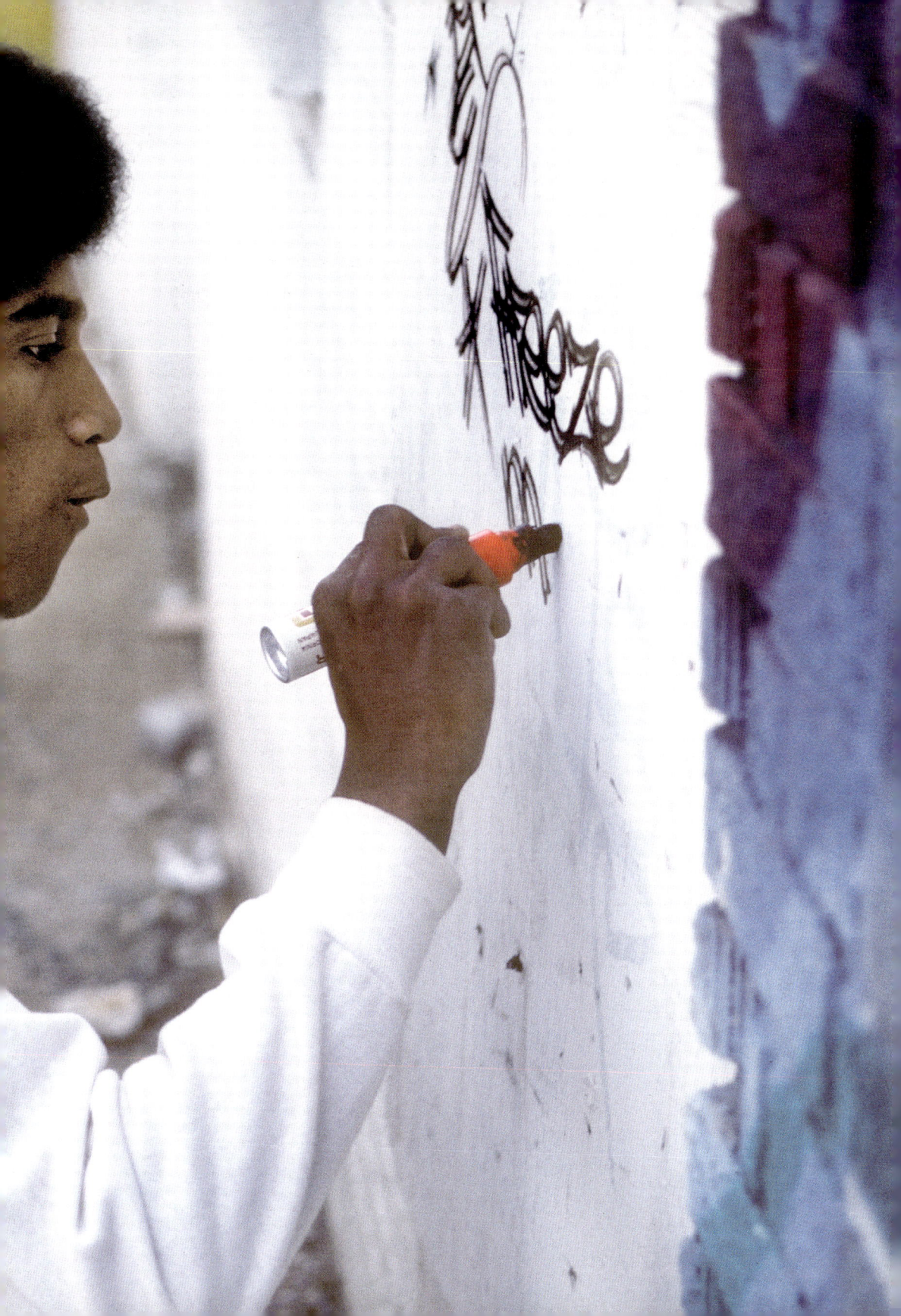

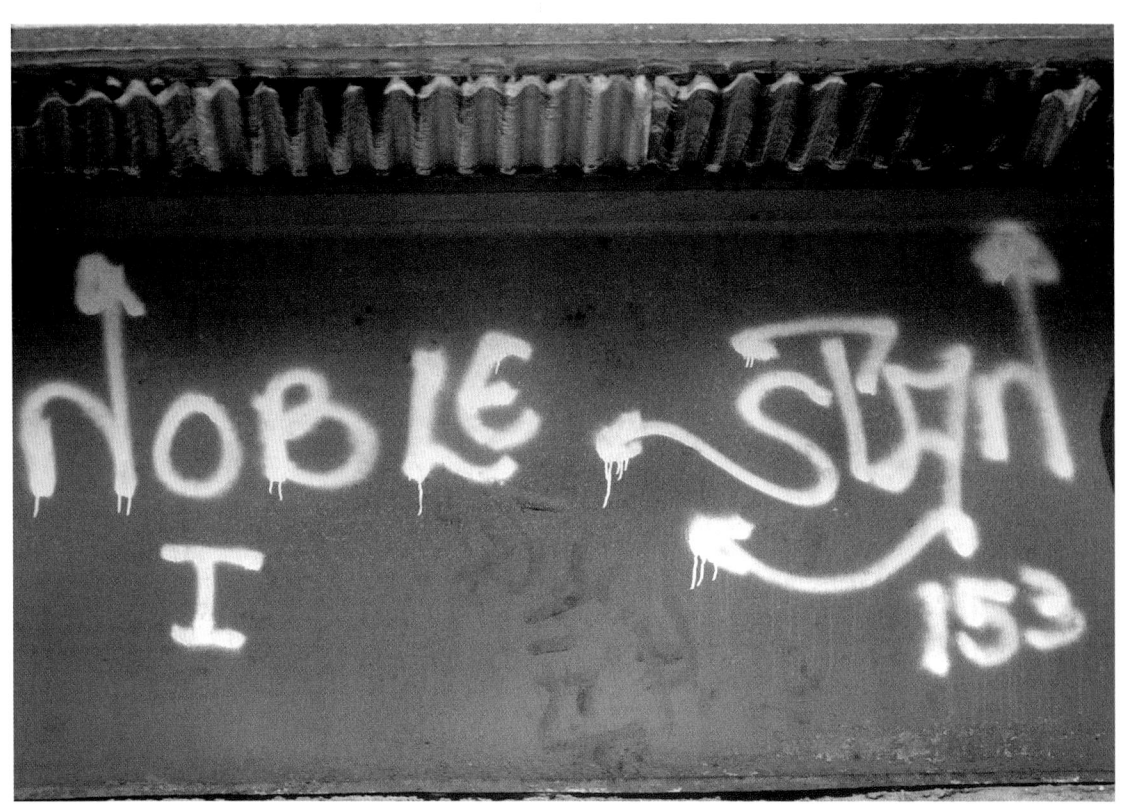

Tools of the Trade – Spraycan

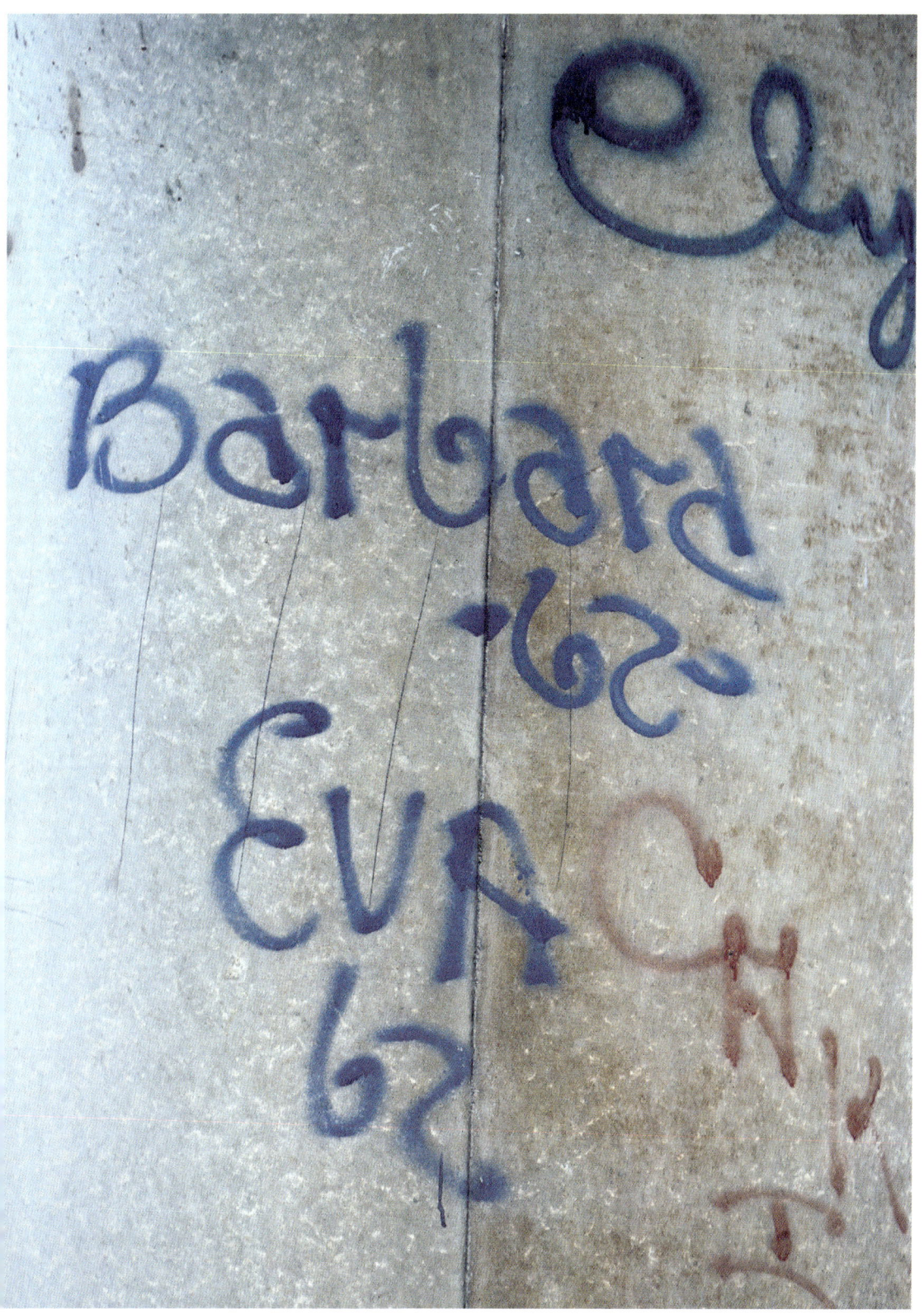

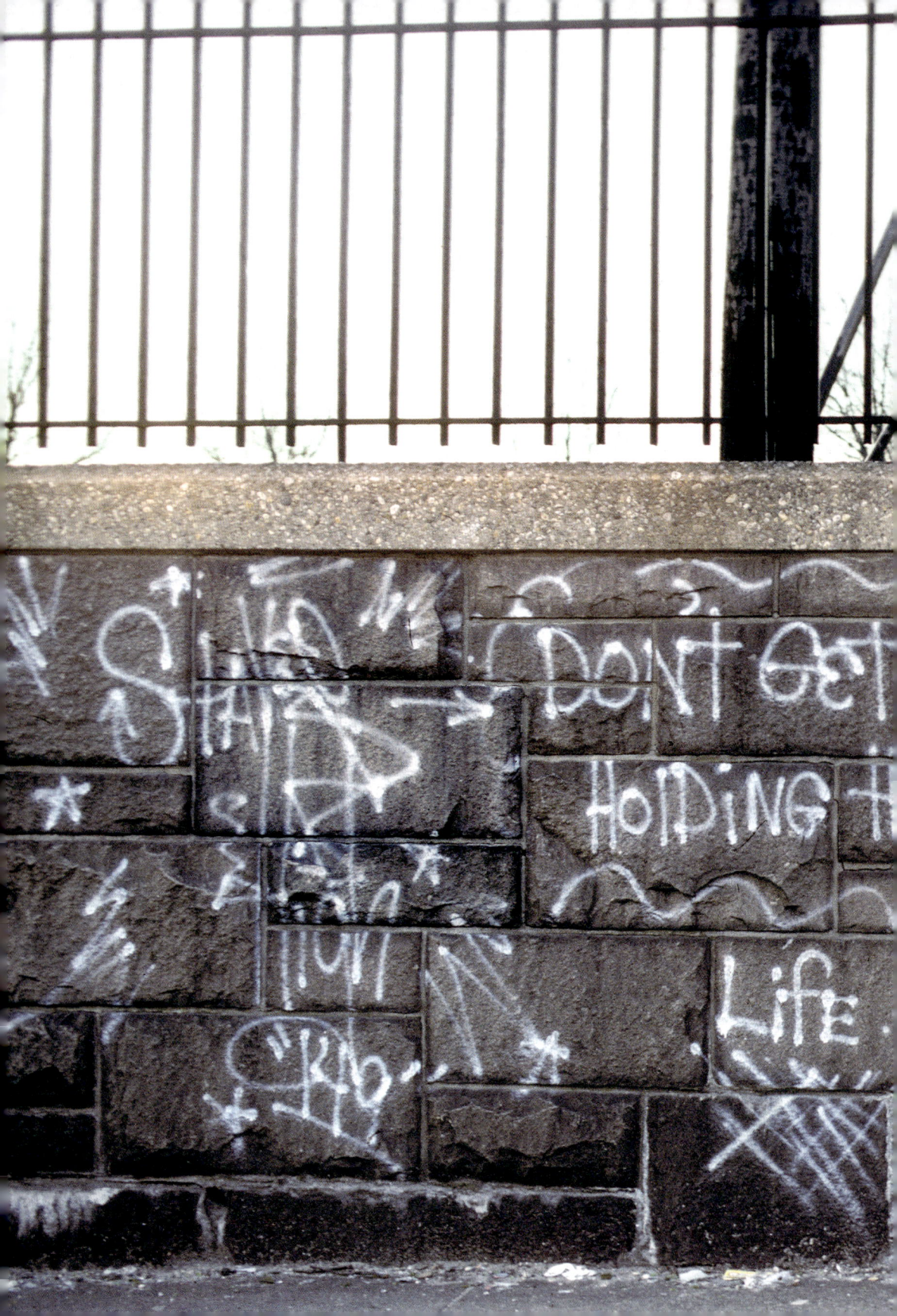

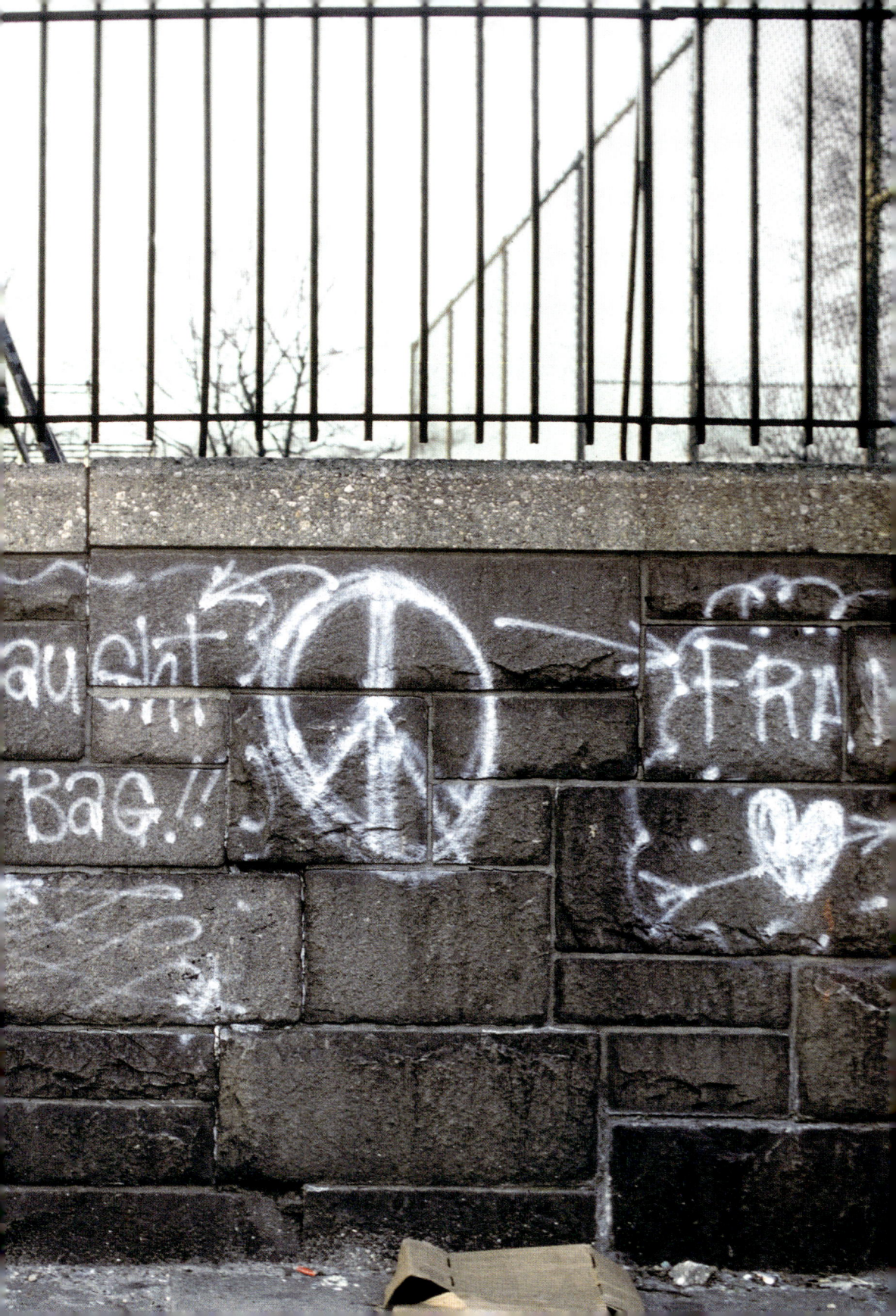

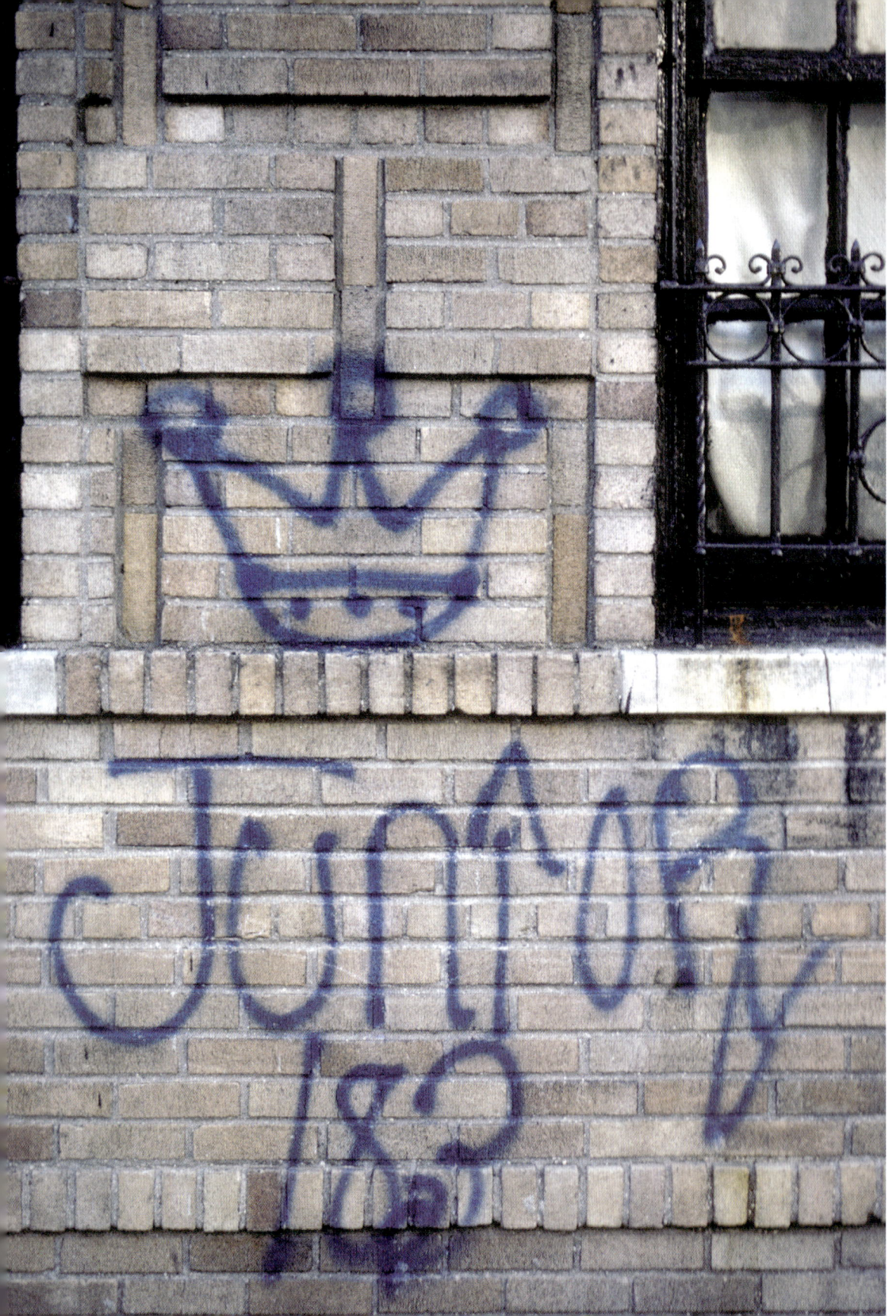

Elements of Style

At first, writers simply wrote their names in their everyday handwriting. However, as tags proliferated, kids wanted their names to stand out. Style is what separated a toy from a skilled writer, and writing with style soon predominated.

By 1973, several different basic styles had developed including a Bronx style, a Brooklyn style, and Broadway Elegant brought to New York from Philadelphia by Top Cat 126. Style could cause conflict as there was a fine line between inspiration and plagiarism. Borrowing from sources such as comics, film and music was acceptable, but biting other writers was taboo.

Kids spent many hours filling countless notebooks practicing their tags, trying to perfect the shape and combination of letters and symbols into a logo that they could repeat quickly. Blade worked hard to design a tag that incorporated several elements.

"Once I finally got it down pat with the Roman number one and the exclamation point all in one motion, it took about ten seconds per hit."

He later added a crown over the tag after other writers began calling him King. An unexpected side effect of being able to write with style was enhanced sex appeal. According to Mare 139, "Love letters were works of art."

Writers embellished their tags with a common set of motifs including crowns, quotation marks, stars, arrows and copyright signs, sometimes with a cloud encircling the whole. Sometimes, for further emphasis, they added a few words such as *Ya Dig!* or *Bad!*. According to Snake 1, the clearest way to make the tag sing was to give it eyes.

Stay High 149 became famous by using a stick figure with a halo derived from the TV series "The Saint", to which he added a smoking joint. Variations by other writers on this theme included stick figures skiing, roller skating, lazing around and wearing a cane and top hat. The saint's halo, has survived by itself to become one of the most characteristic symbols used in tags today.

Style often obscures the letter forms in tags, making them illegible to the uninitiated. Recognizing styles and deciphering the handwriting is like solving a puzzle. The reward is in discovering a fresh sense of design and gaining a better understanding of one's surroundings.

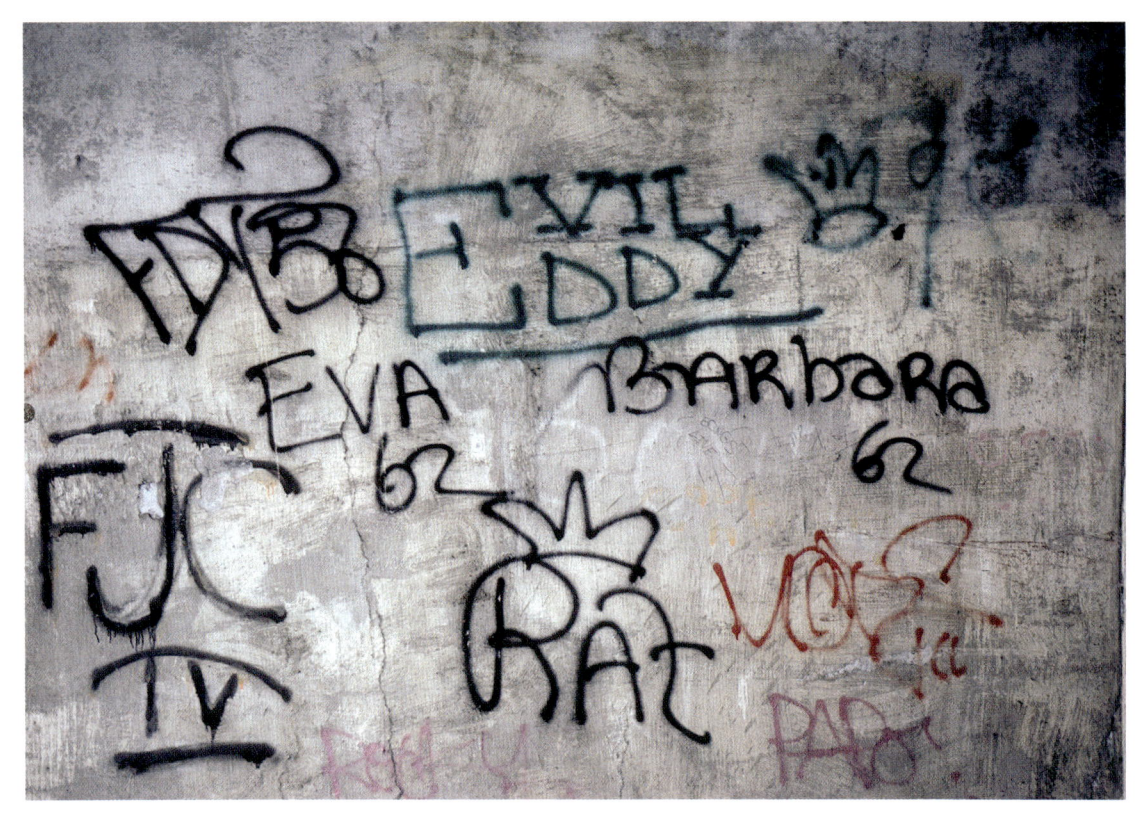

Elements of Style – Evil Eddie Types

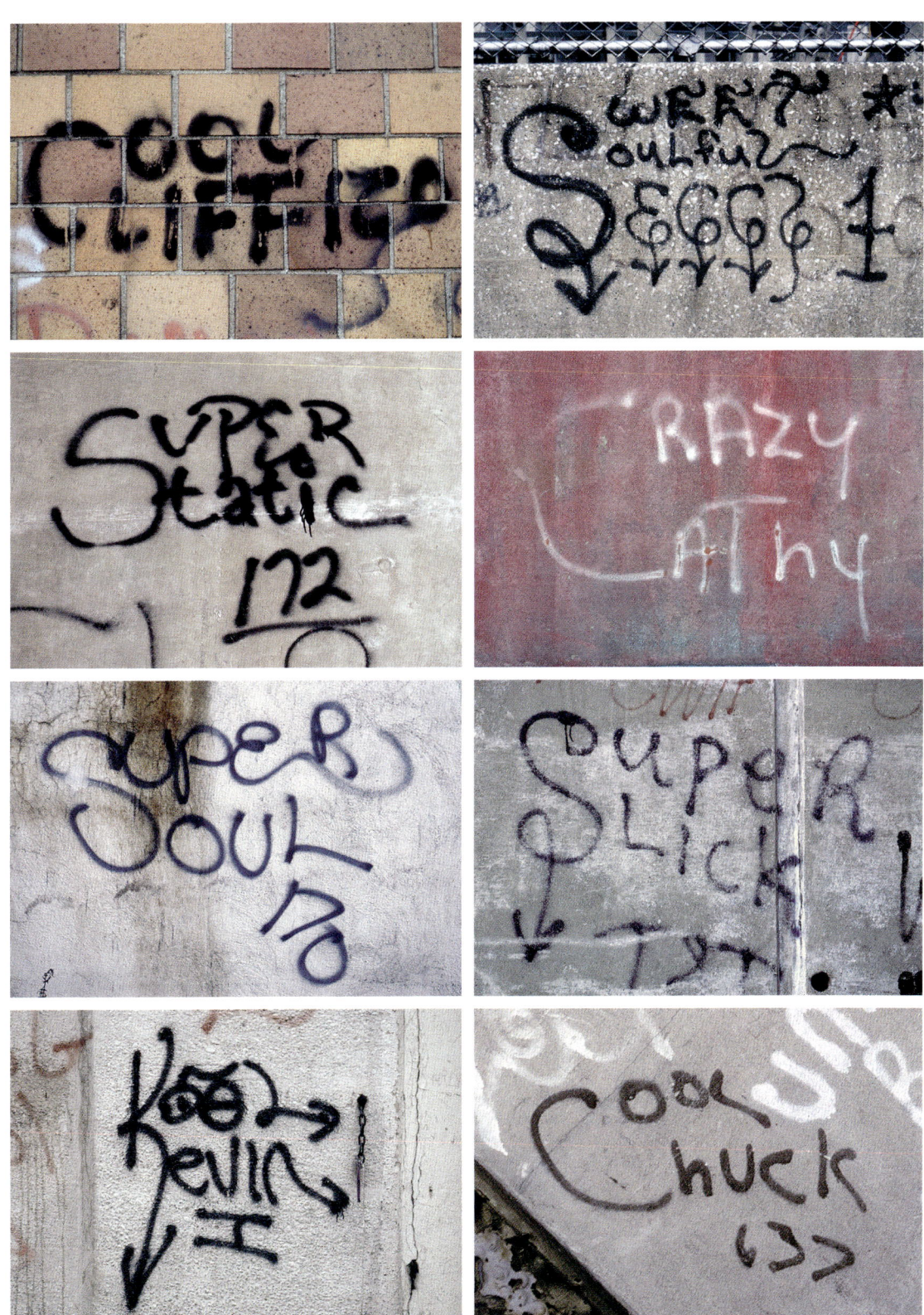

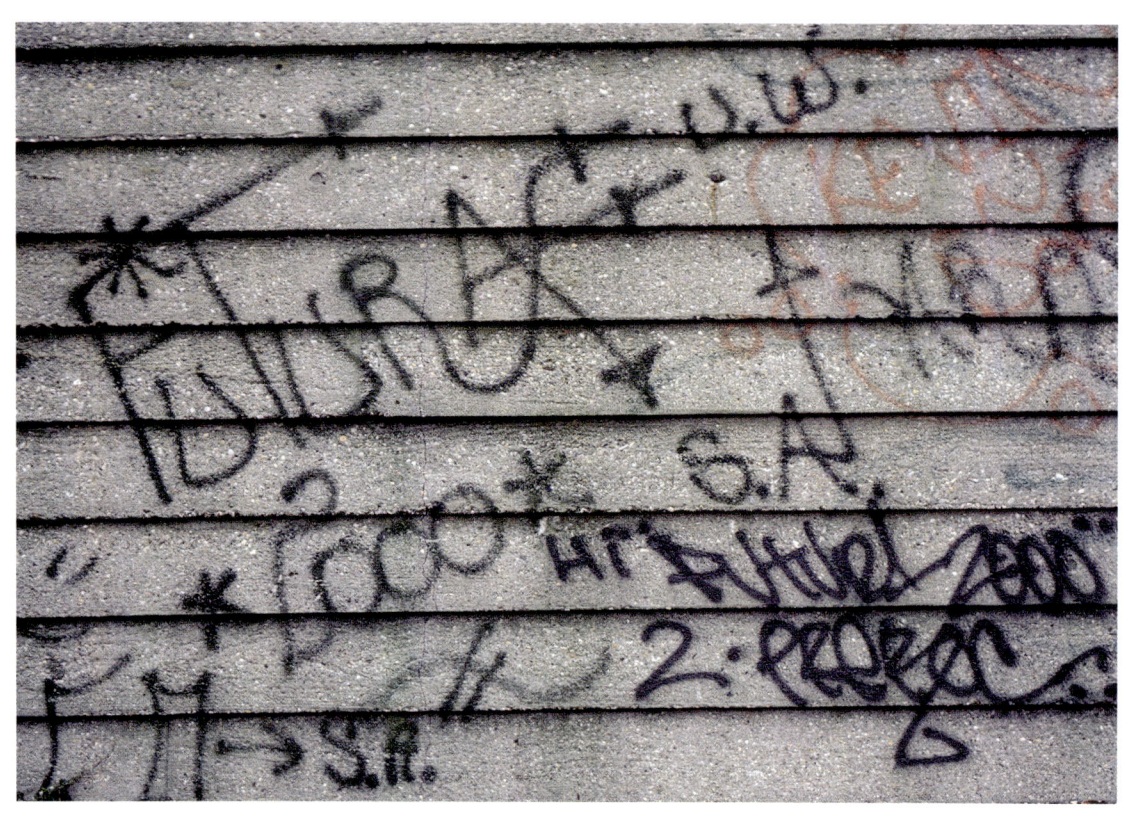

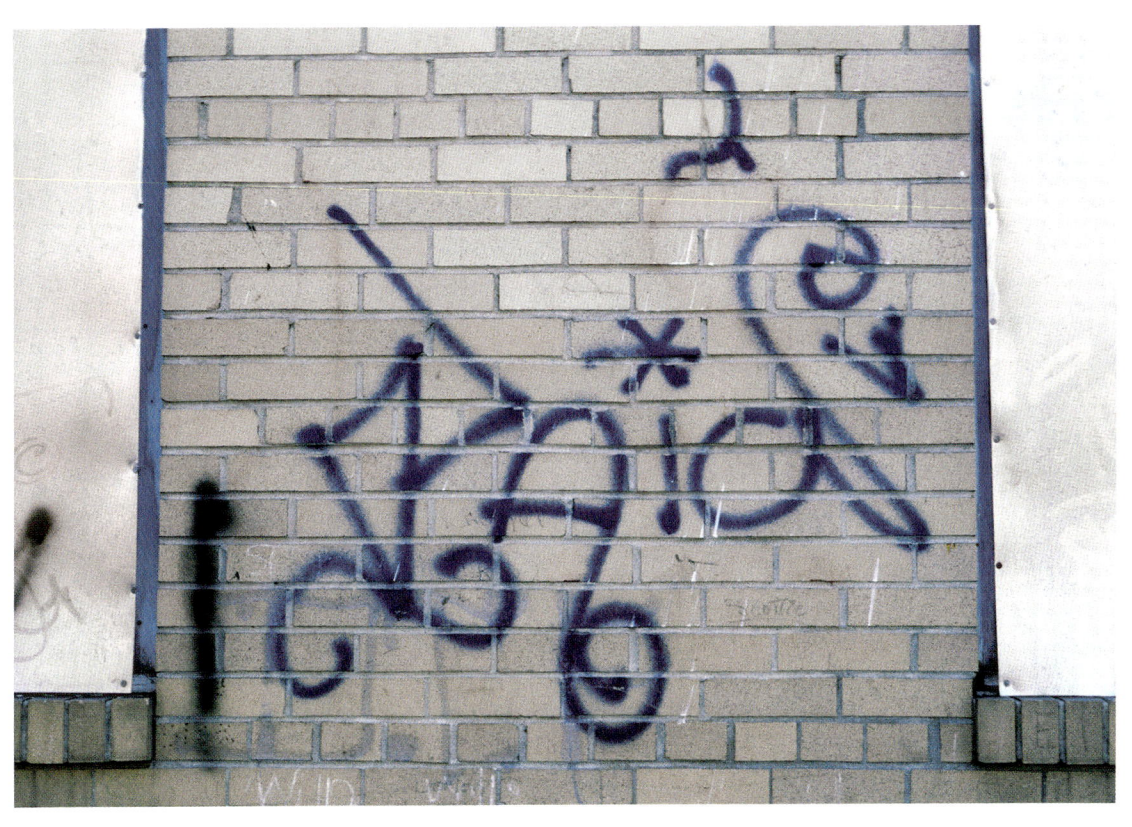

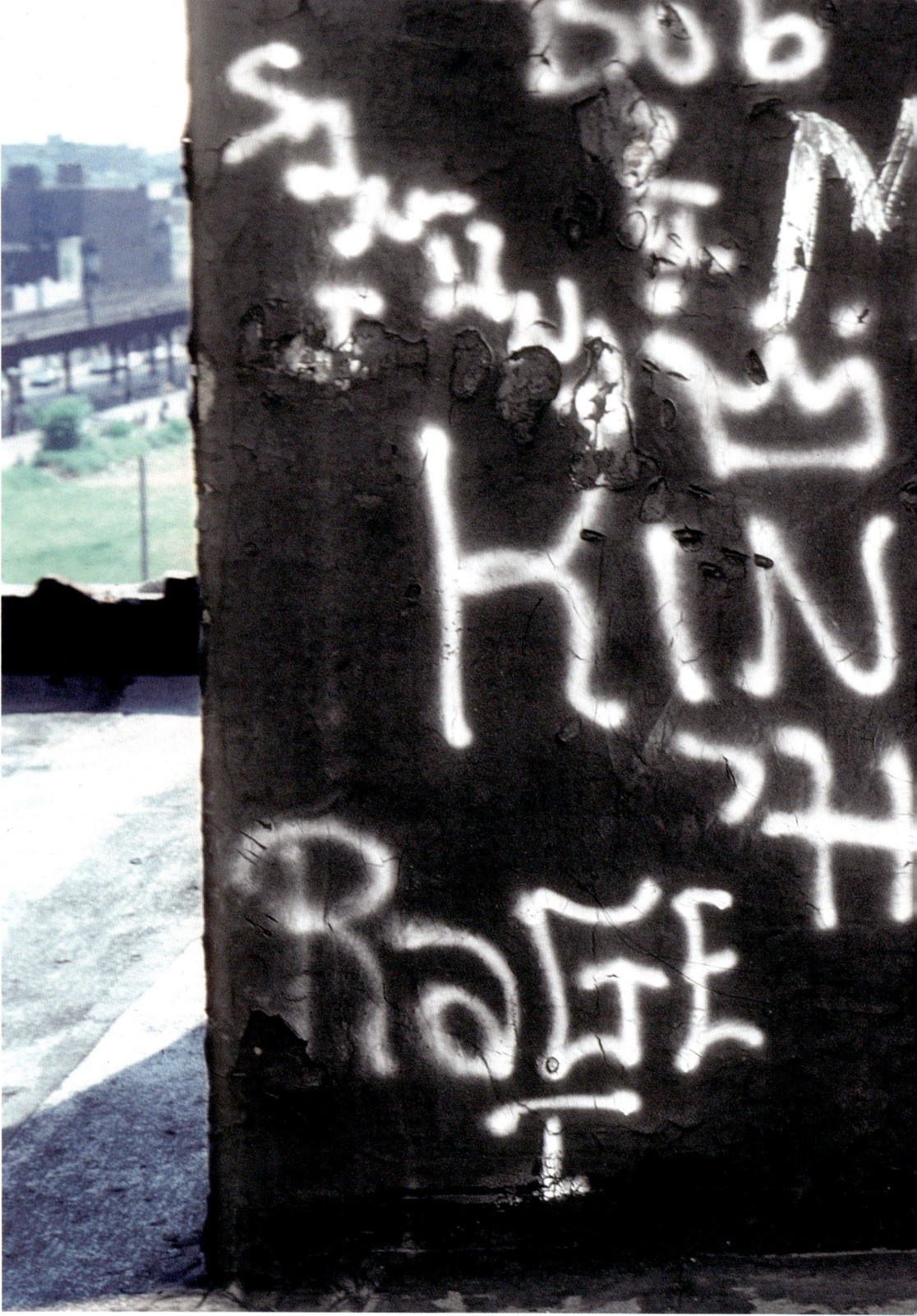

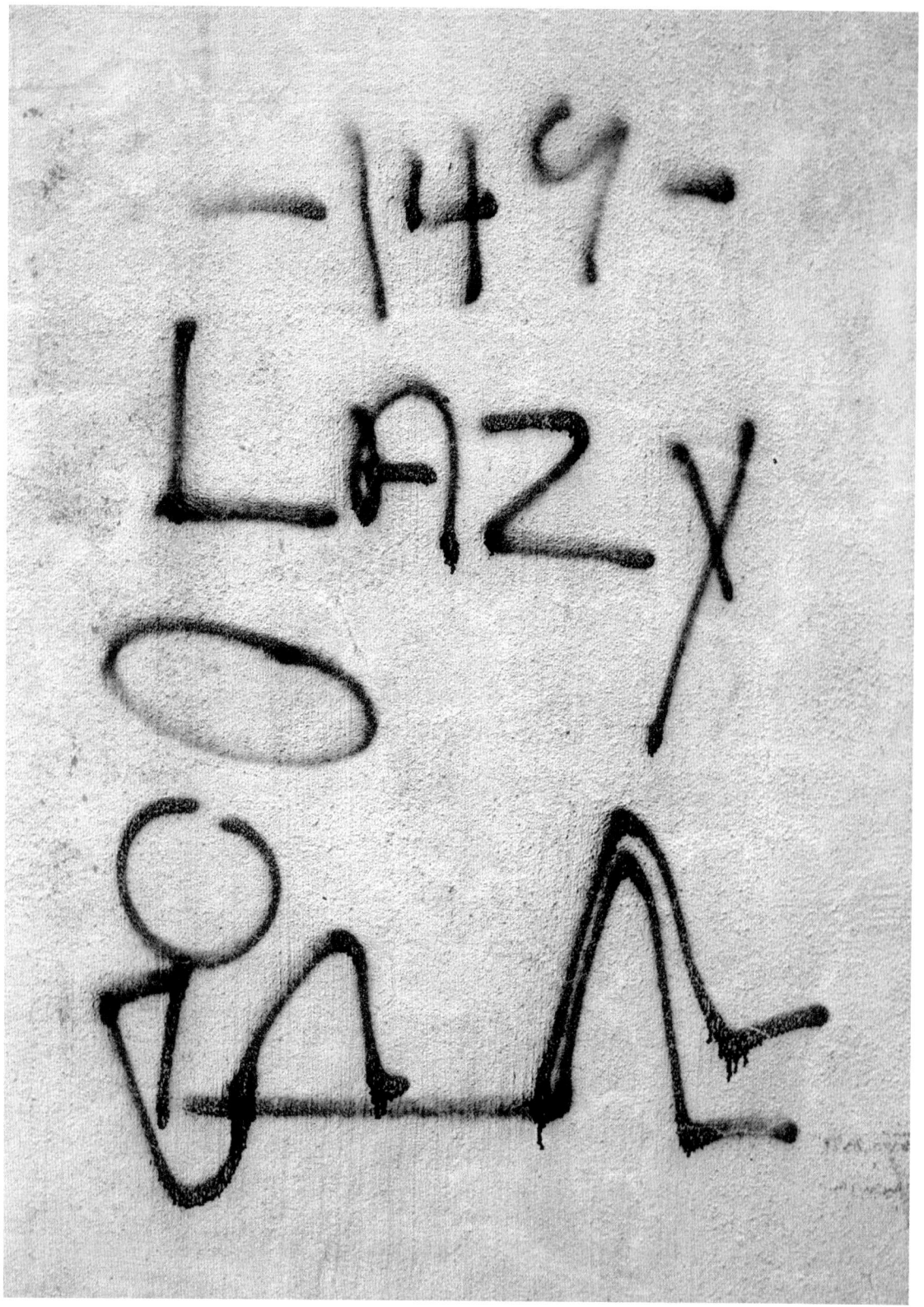

Elements of Style – Stick Figures

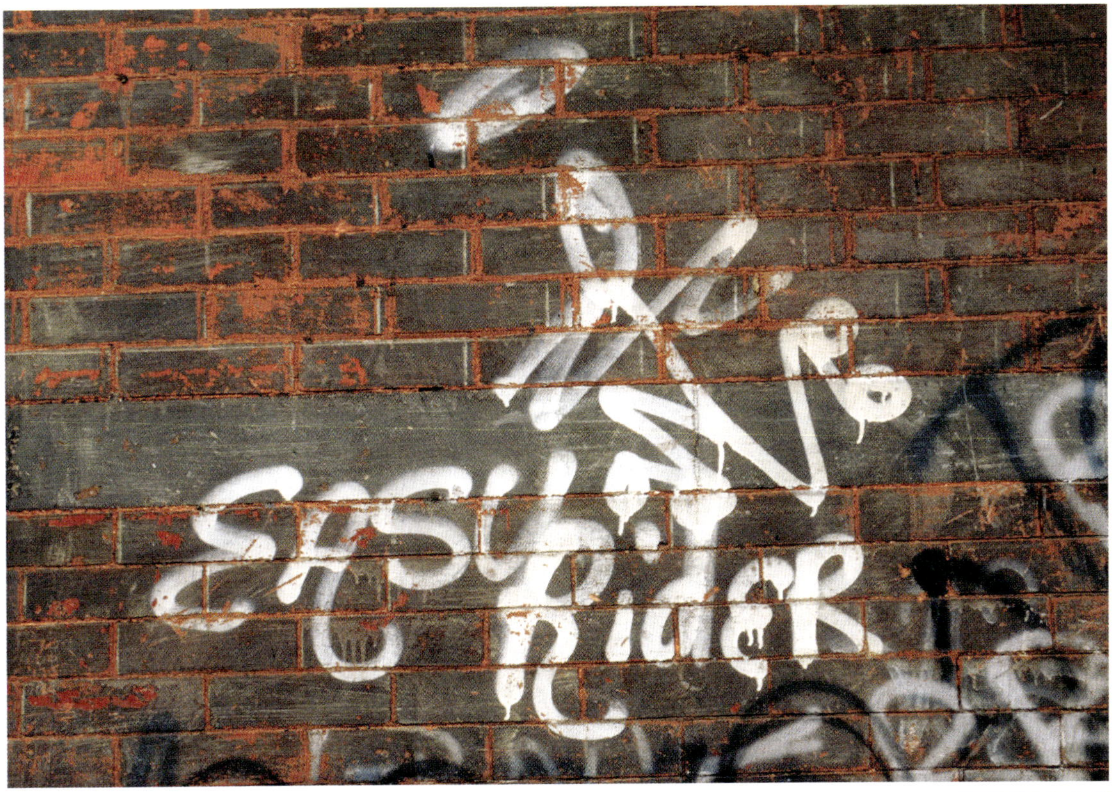

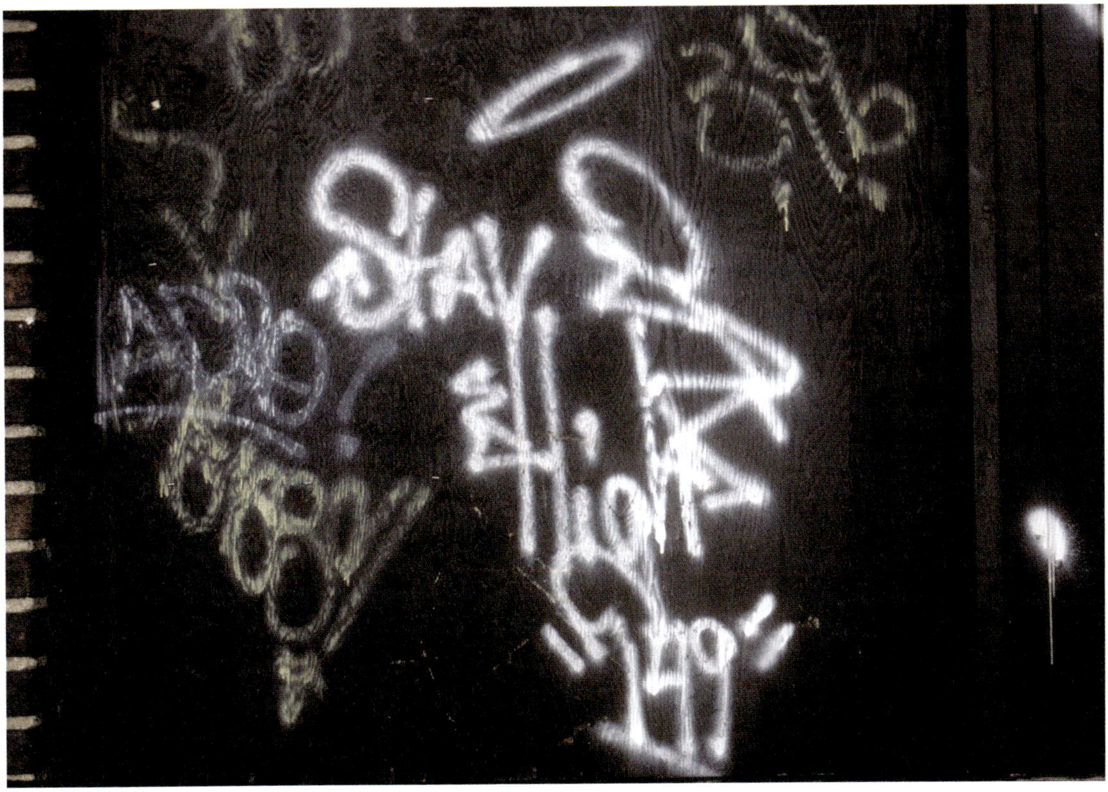

Elements of Style – Stick Figures

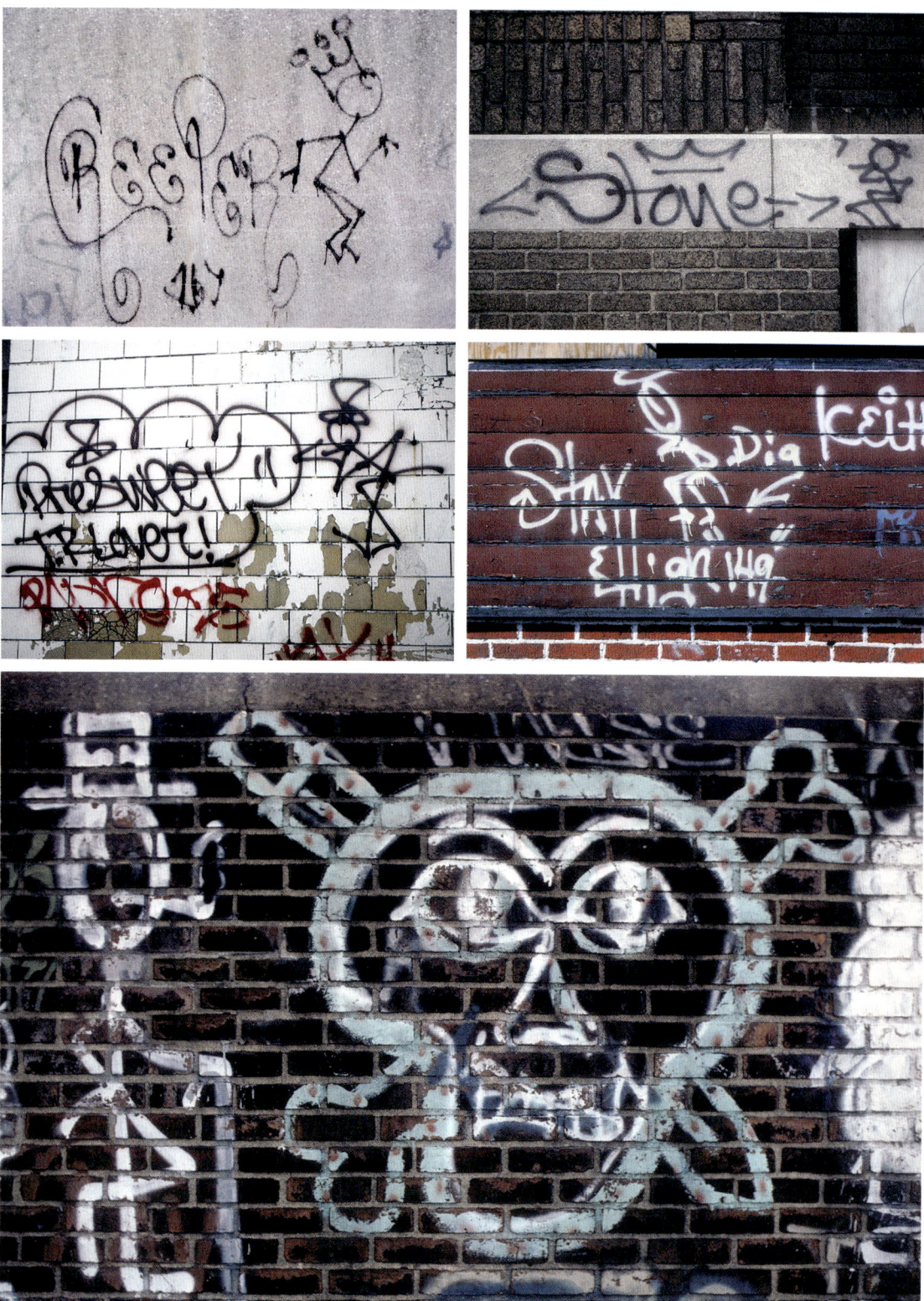

Elements of Style – Stick Figures

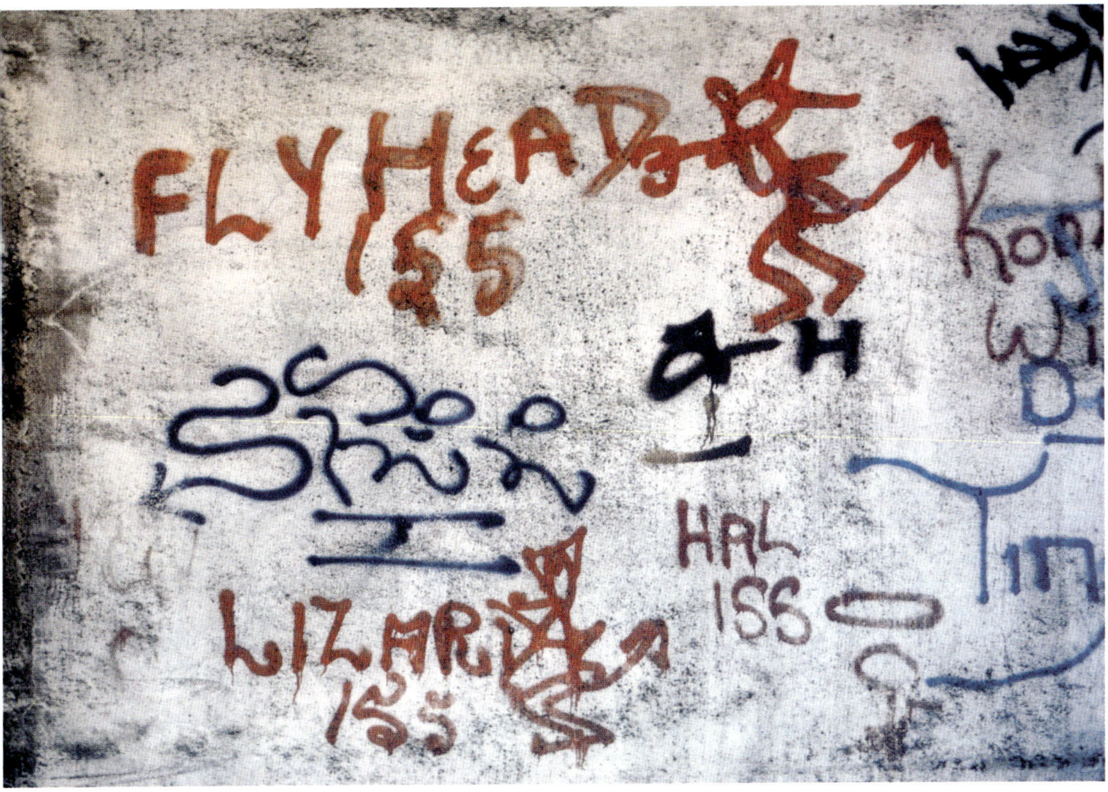

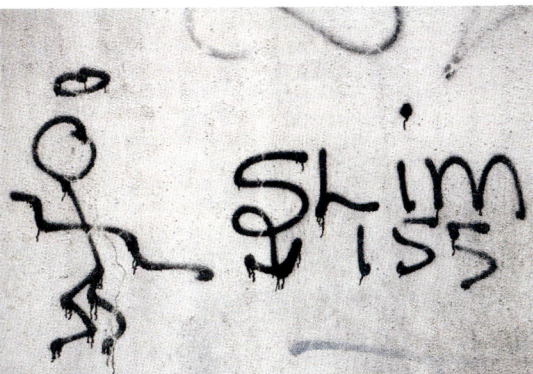

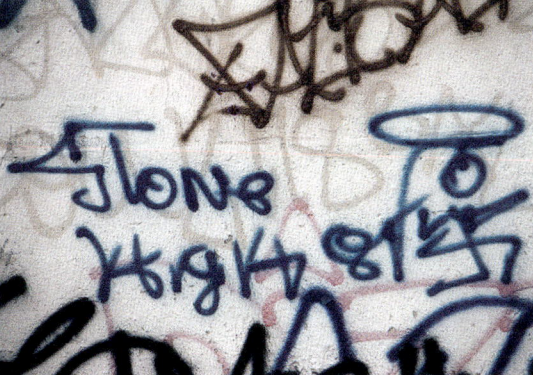

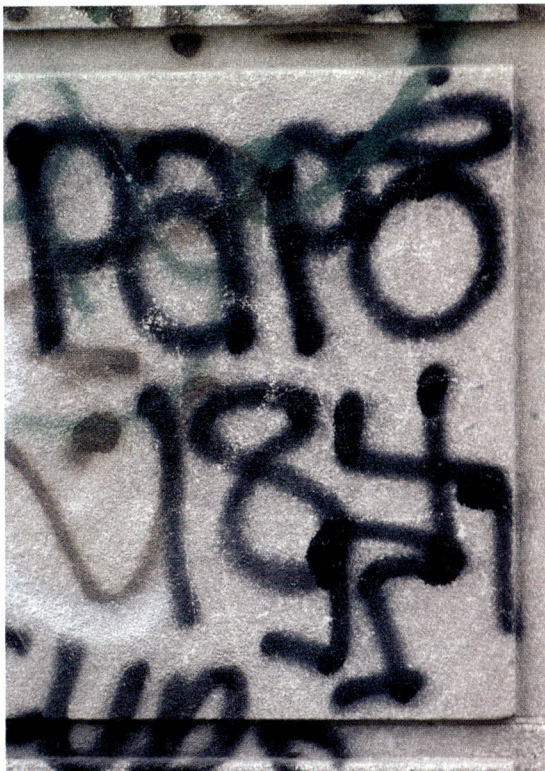

Elements of Style – Stick Figures

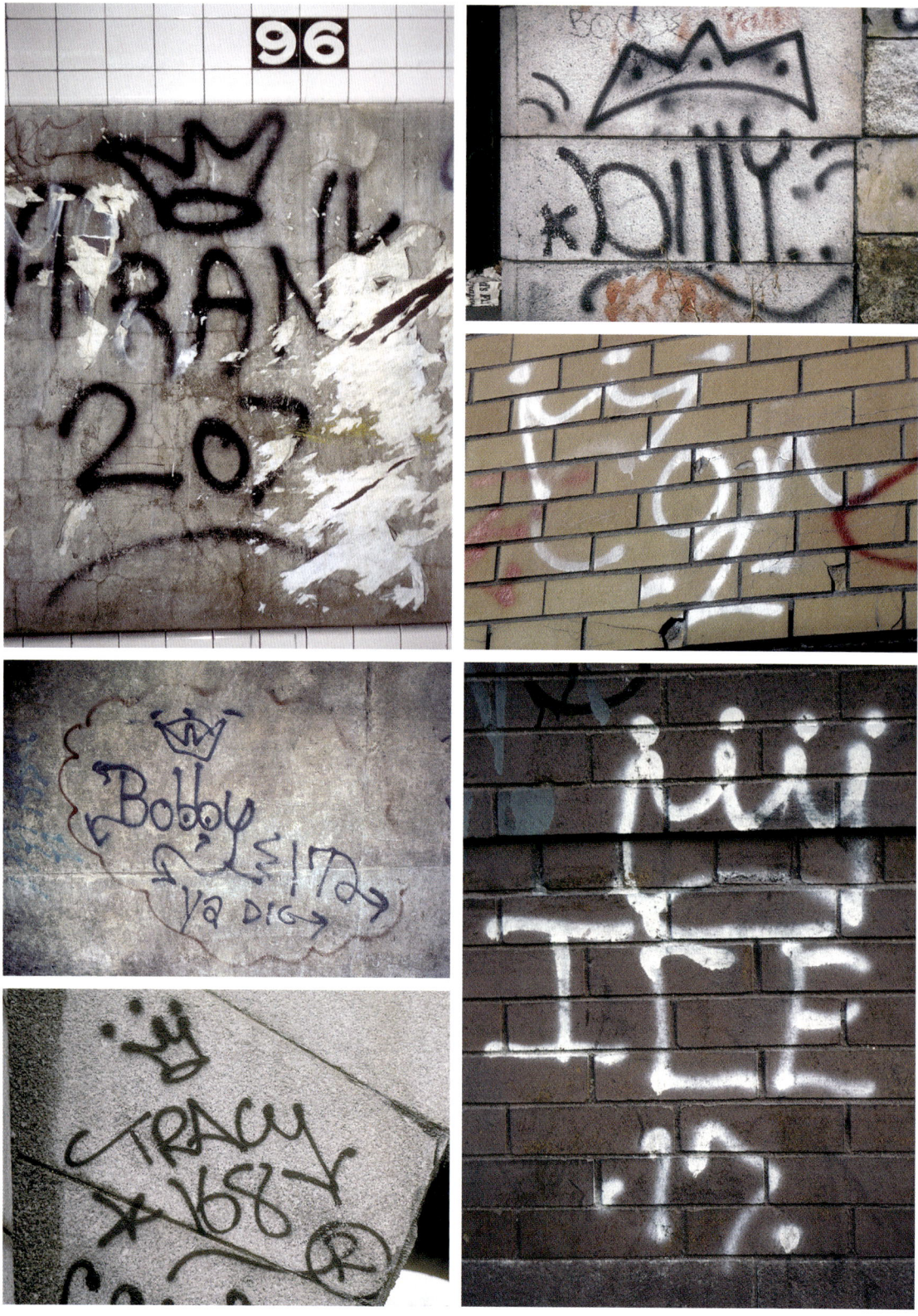

Elements of Style – Crowns

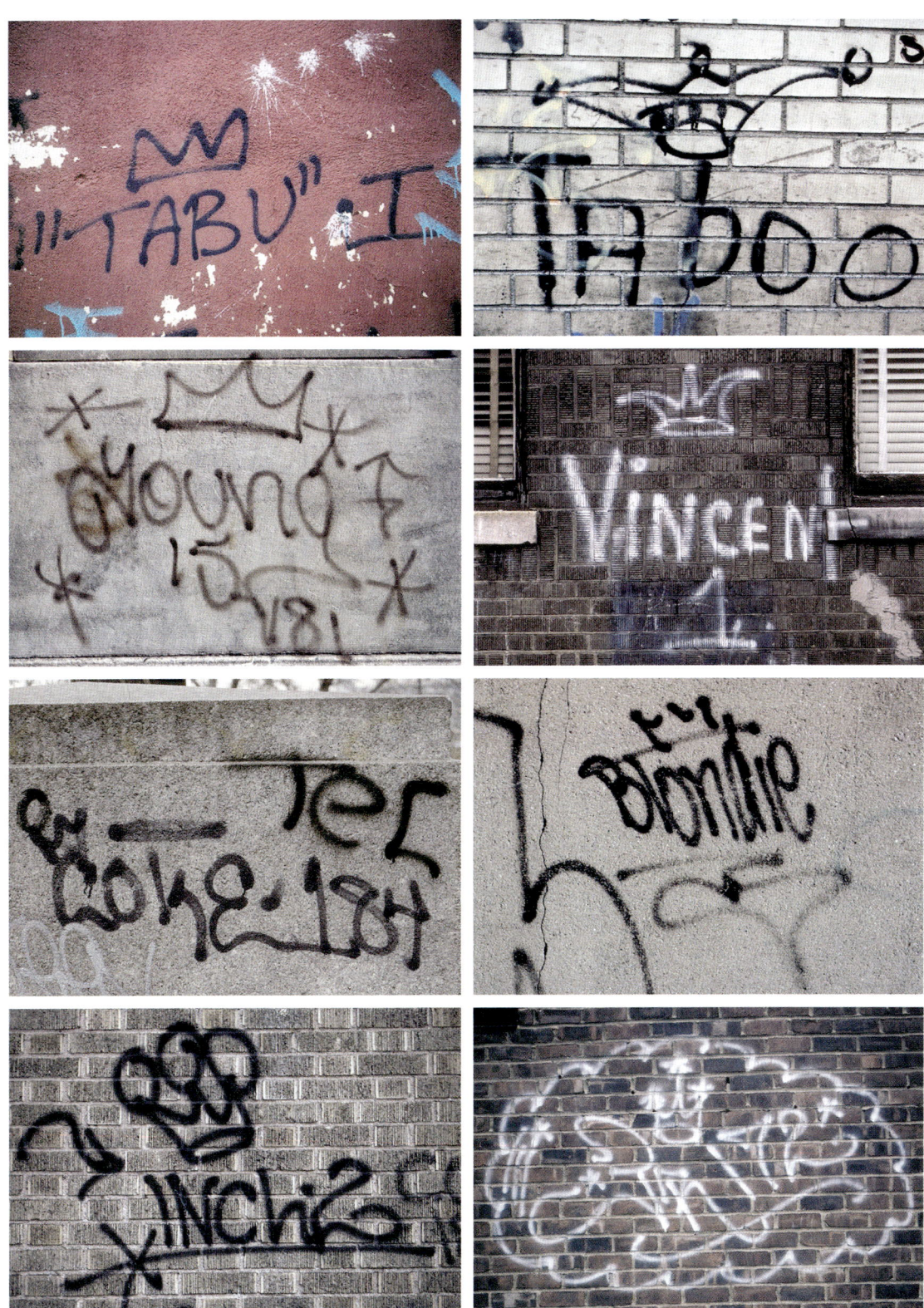

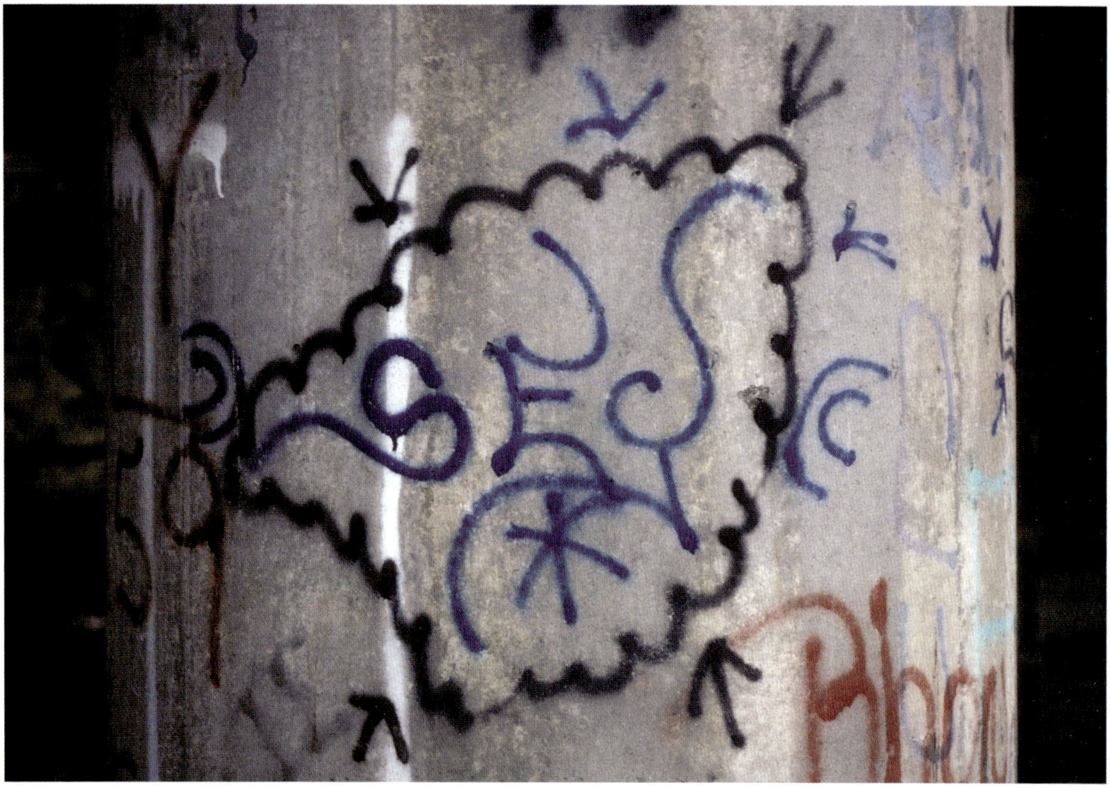

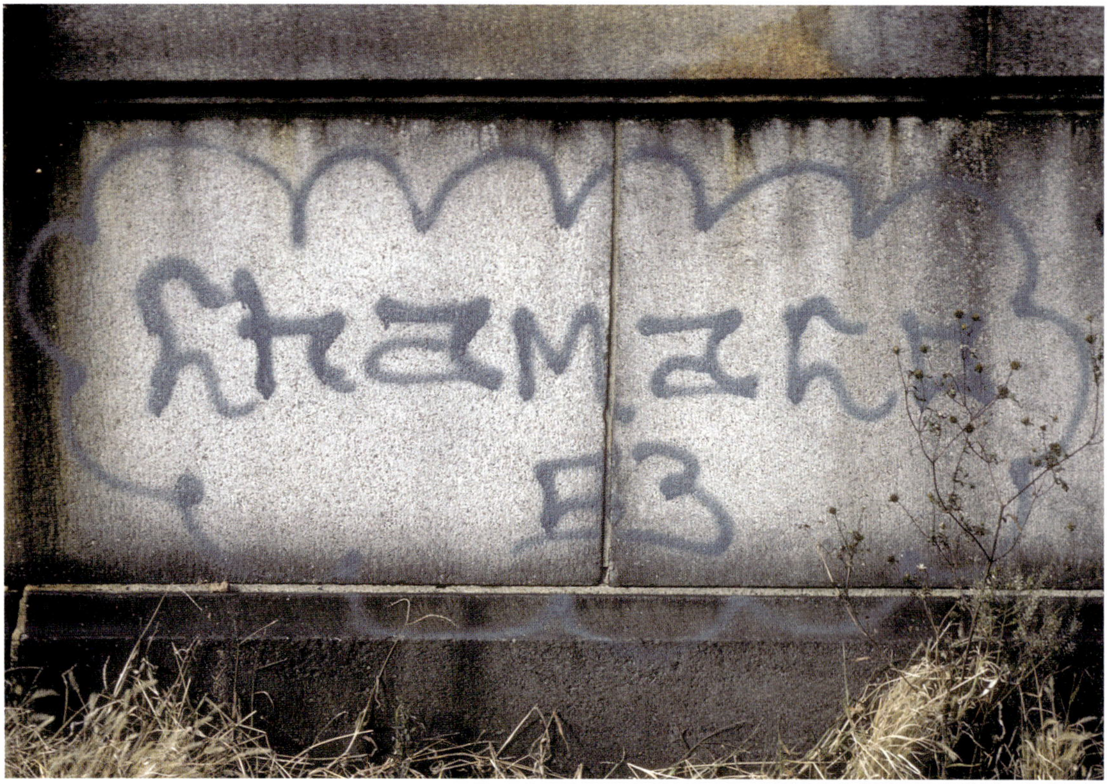

Elements of Style – Clouds

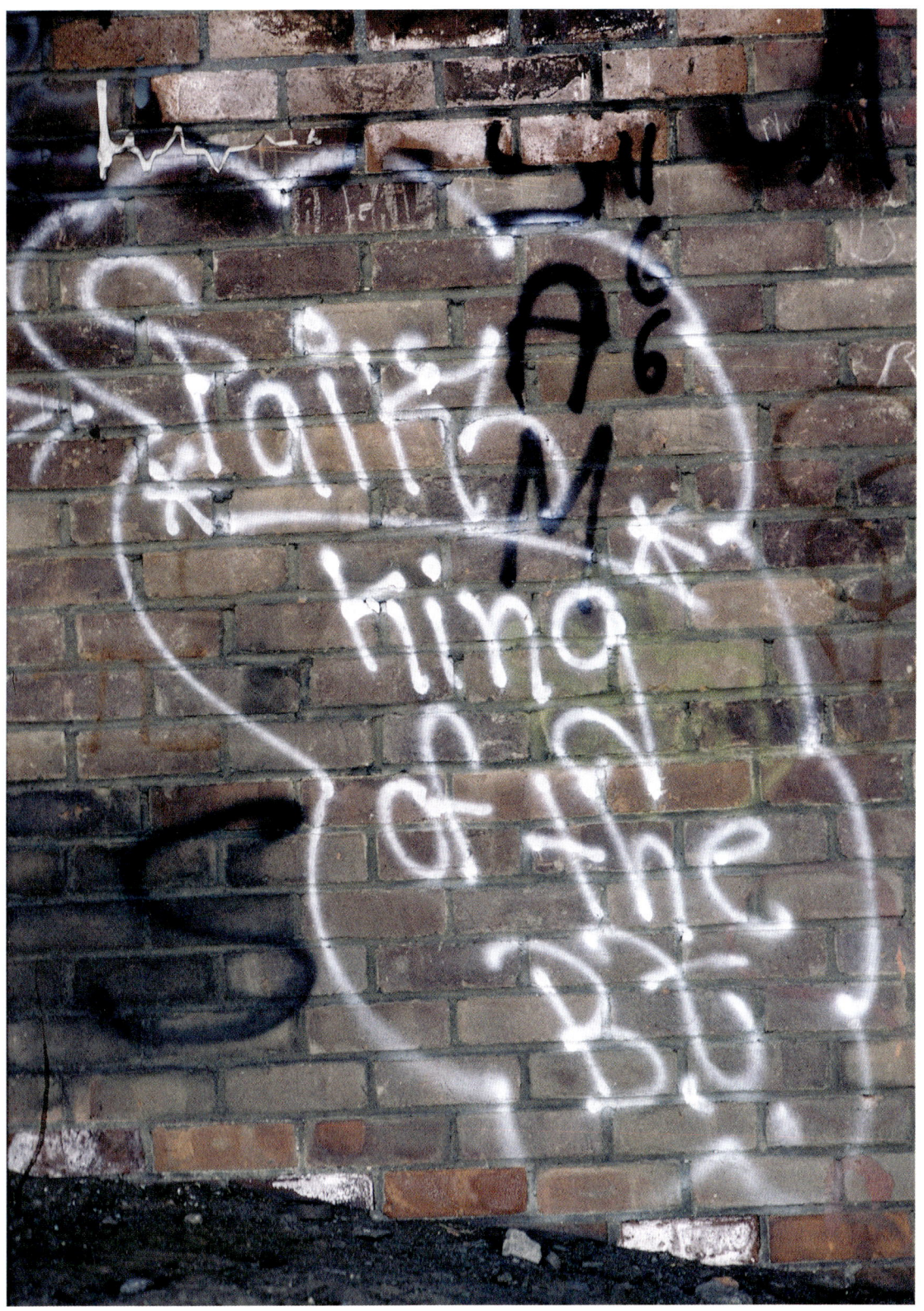

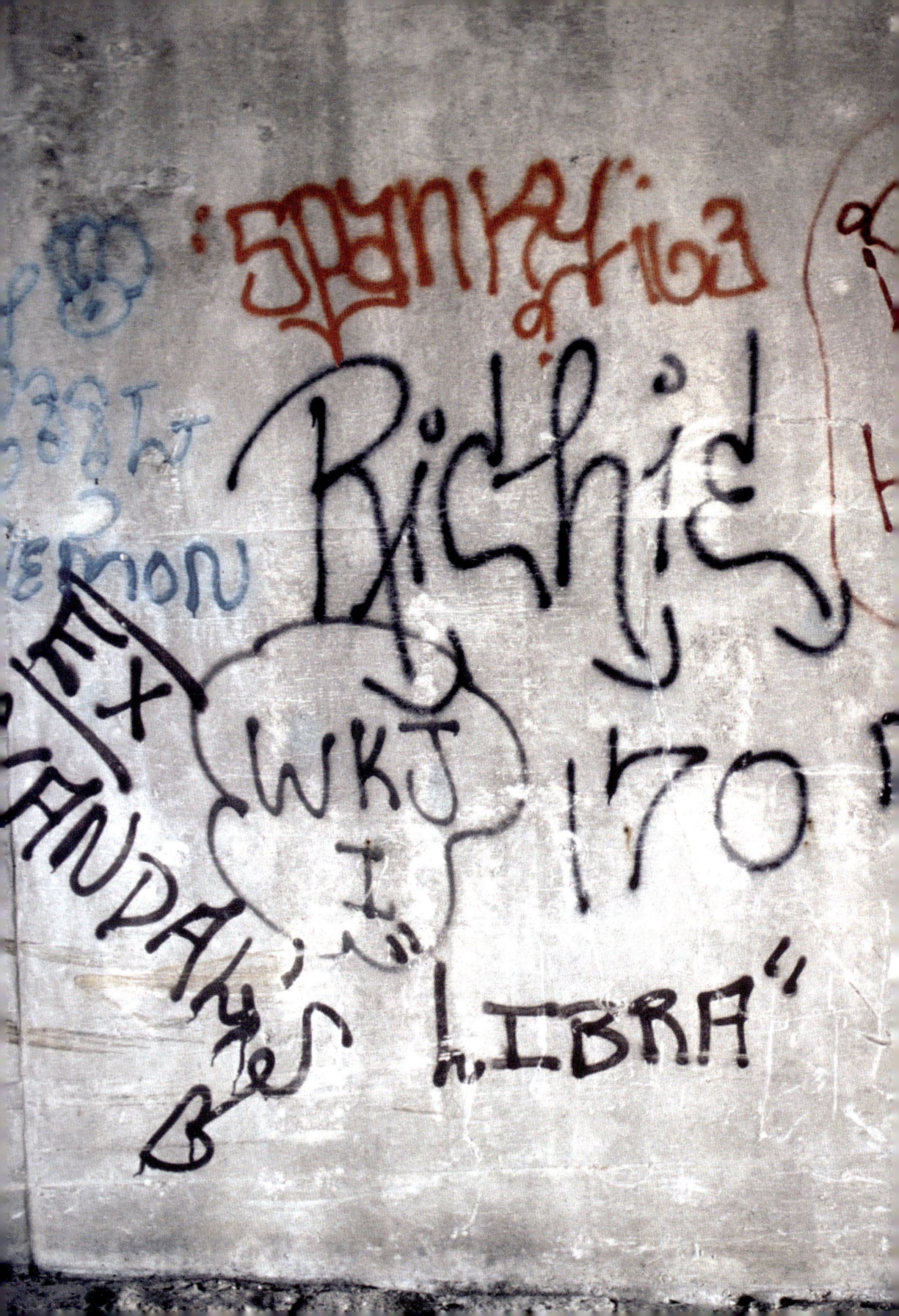

"5panky163

Richie

EX
VANDAL
WKJ
170
LIBRA"

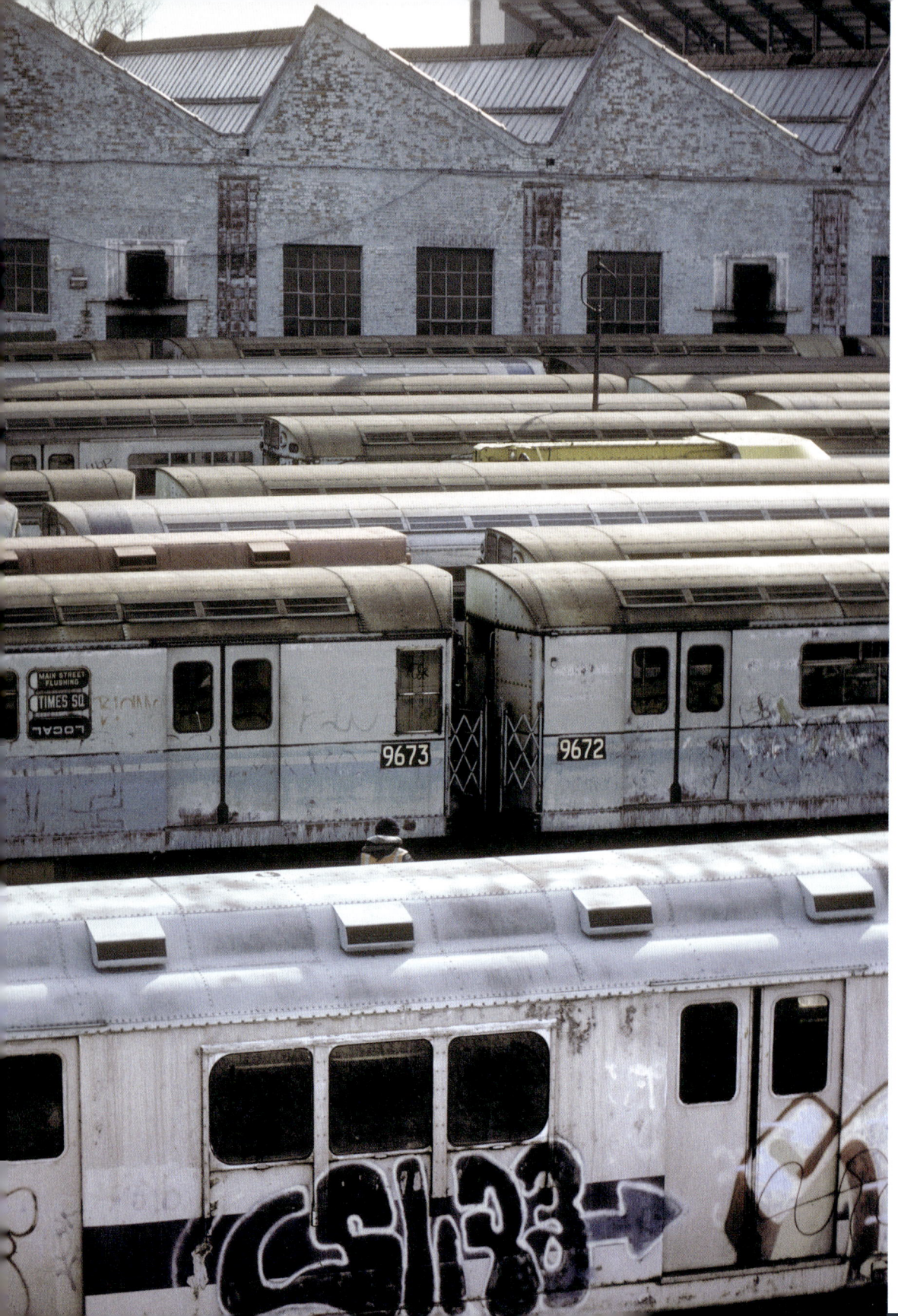

Early Pieces

The earliest pieces were simply tags outlined in a contrasting color. When kids found they could use the wide-spraying nozzles of fat caps to fill large areas with paint quickly, their graffiti pieces soon covered entire walls and subway cars. The combination of spray paint and trains led to swift stylistic development. By 1973 they were using the subway system to wage a style war. Writers numbered in the thousands, and graffiti spread across New York and beyond. By the mid 70s, letters had evolved into complex wildstyle pieces. Painted trains traveled from the Bronx, through Manhattan and out to the far reaches of Brooklyn. Writers eagerly studied pieces on trains and incorporated stylistic innovations from other boroughs.

Although authorities considered tags a nuisance, they ignored graffiti until the subway became the primary goal of writers. Even the Metropolitan Transit Authority failed to react as there was no city law on the books. Writing on trains or subway stations was simply an infringement of the MTA's rules. Youngsters who were caught got off with a warning, while those over sixteen were just charged with malicious mischief.

In 1972 Mayor John Lindsay passed the first anti-graffiti law. It stipulated that no person could write, paint or draw inscriptions, shapes or marks of any kind on public property. It became illegal to carry spray paint in public buildings unless the container was sealed. He ordered that writers be sentenced to remove graffiti. The law was not particularly effective as writers used these cleaning sessions to plan new exploits.

The public grew increasingly angry about tagging, an activity they regarded as symbolizing a city out of control. Many made a distinction between graffiti art and vandalism, and tagging always fell into the latter category. However a close look at any large graffiti mural will reveal elements of letter design and motifs such as crowns, arrows and stars that were already present in the earliest tags and pieces.

Not everyone hated graffiti. In 1973 in New York Magazine, artist Claes Oldenburg enthusiastically endorsed graffiti as an appropriate New York City phenomenon. "You're standing there in the station, everything is gray and gloomy, and all of a sudden one of those graffiti trains slides in and brightens the place like a big bouquet from Latin America. At first it seems anarchial – makes you wonder if the subways are working properly. Then you get used to it. The city is like a newspaper anyway, so it's natural to see writing all over the place."

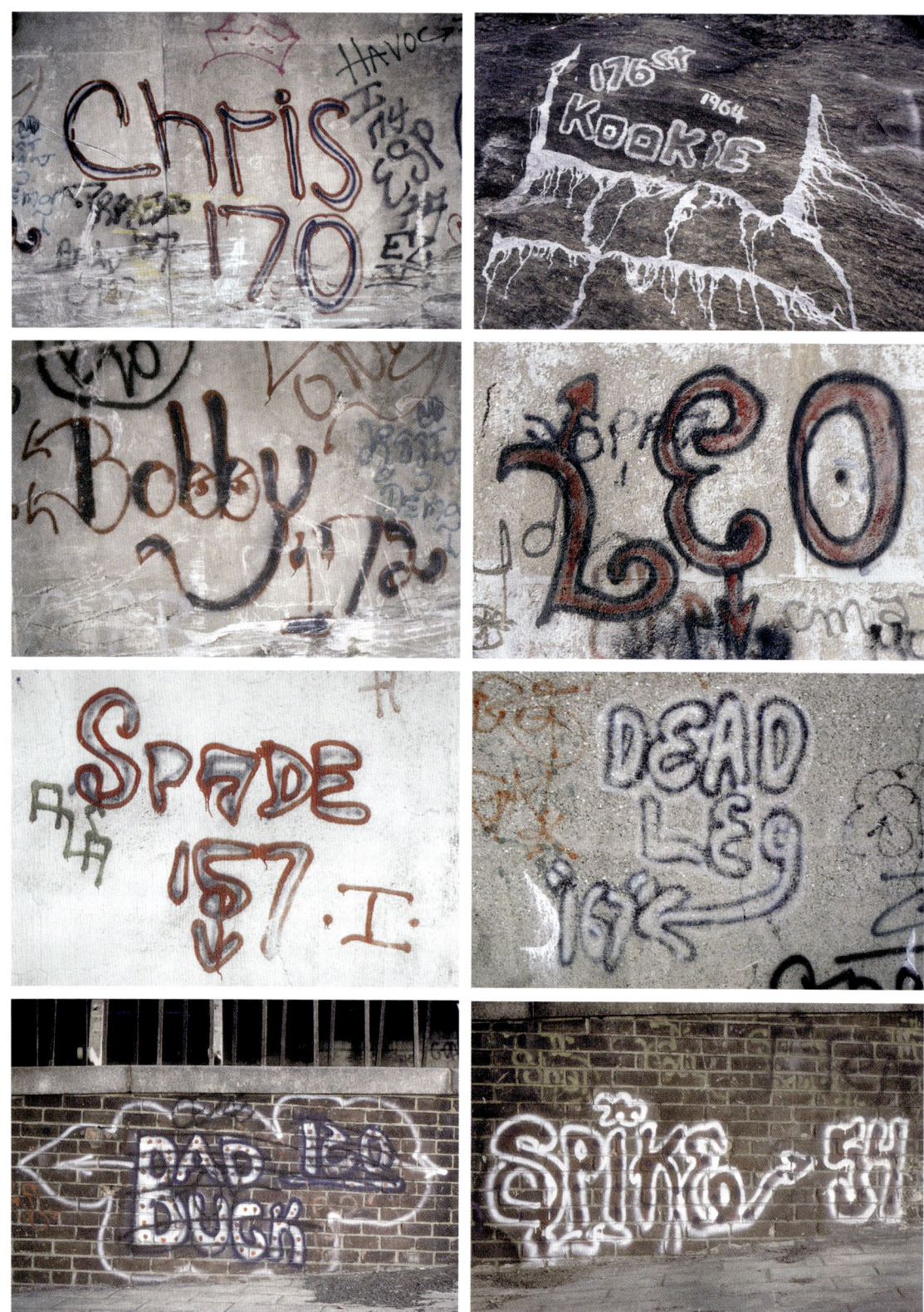

Early Pieces – Tags with Outlines

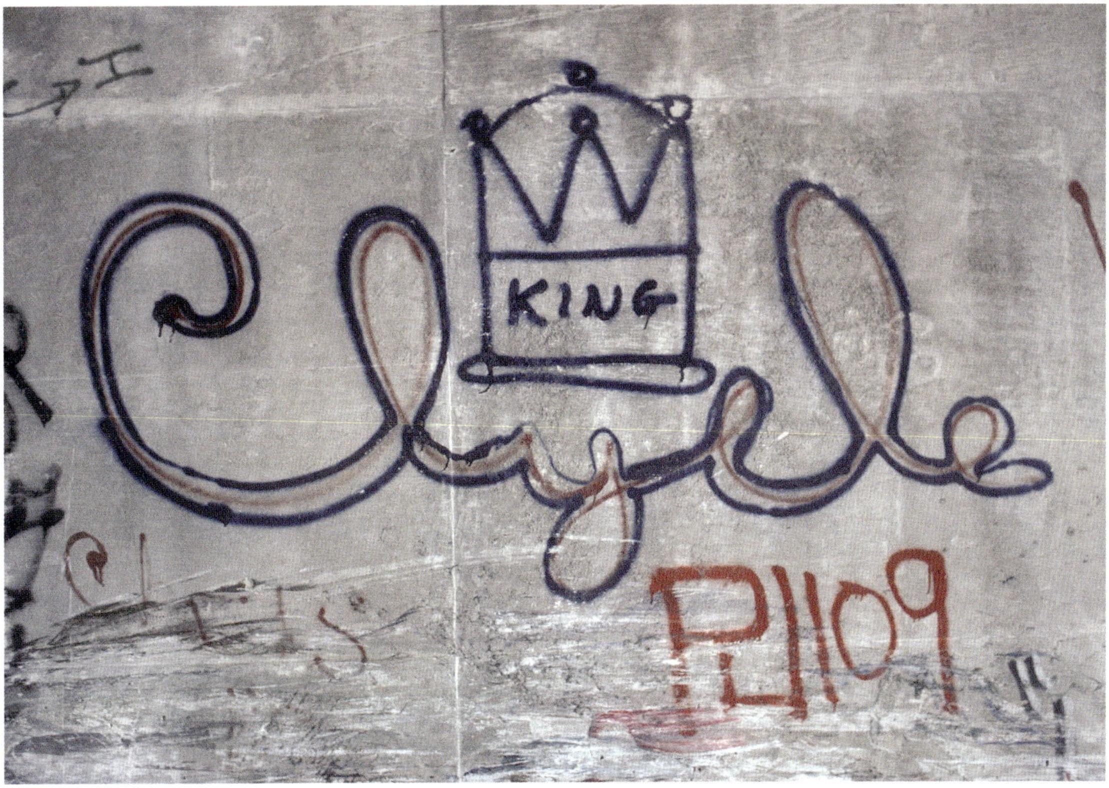
KING

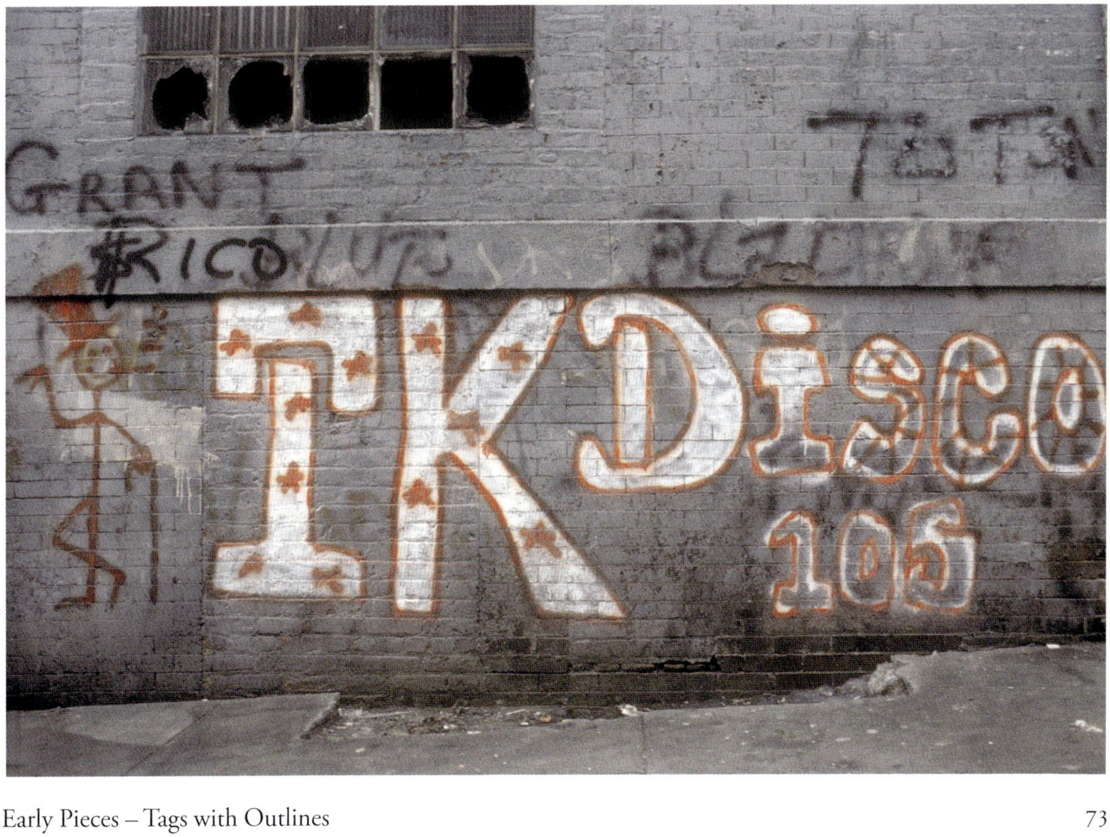
GRANT
RICO
TK Disco
105

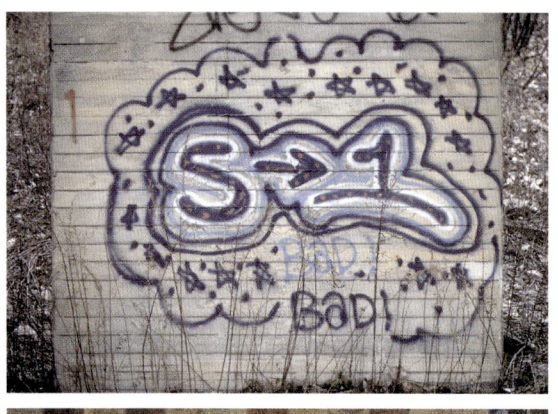
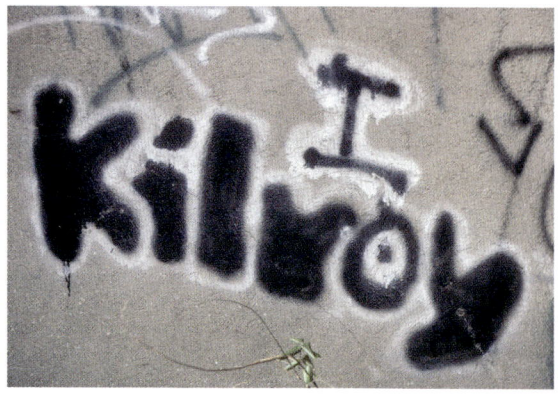
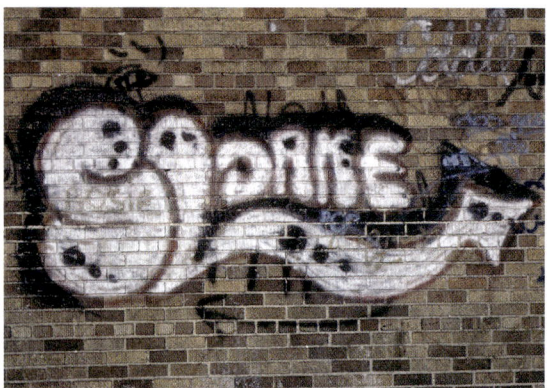
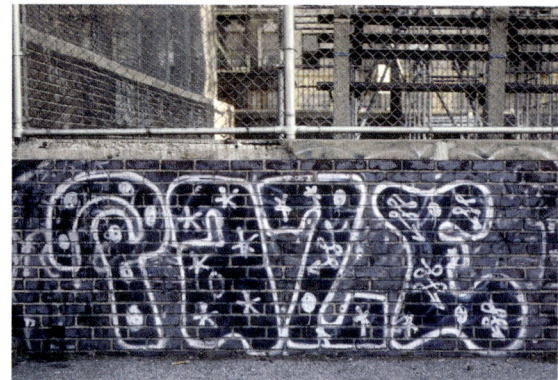

Early Pieces – Various Styles

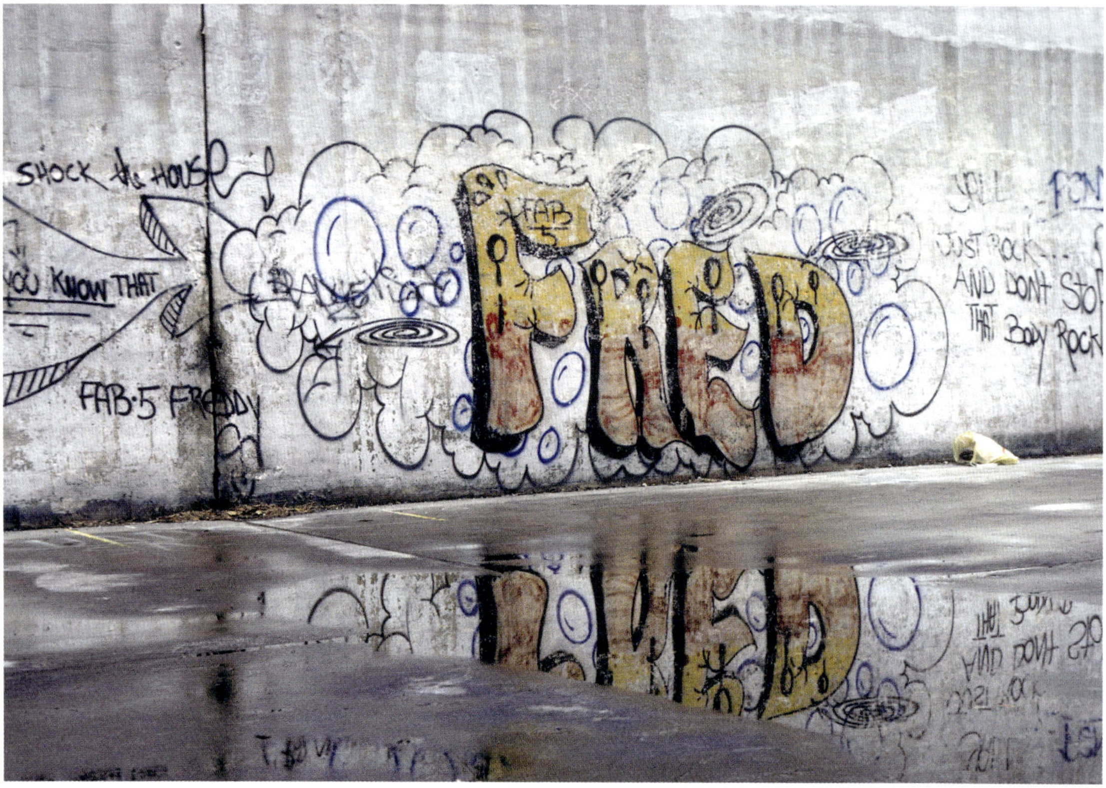

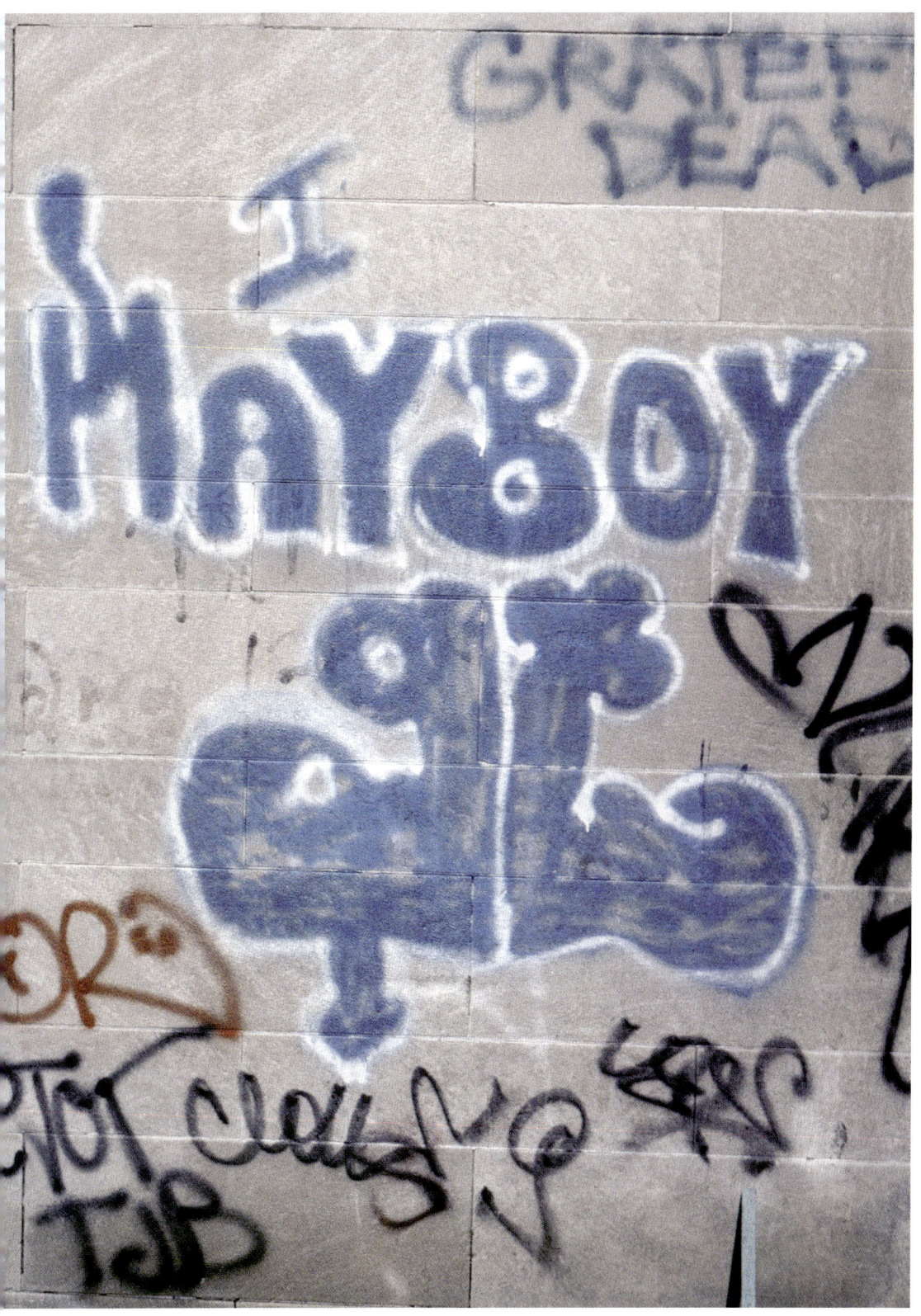

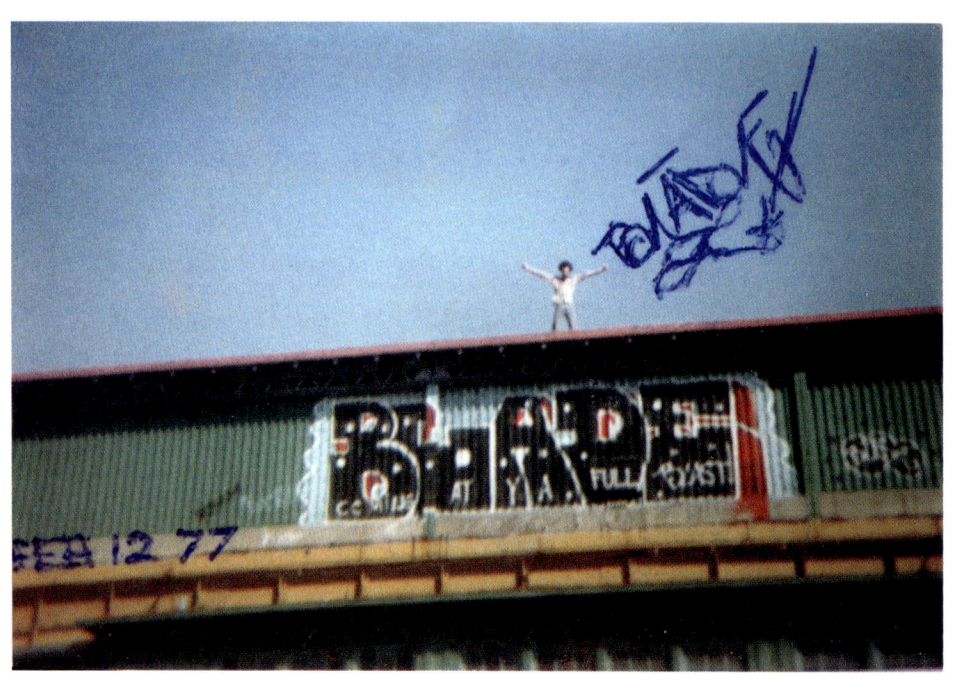

I'M STANDING ON THE ROOF OF
BURKE AVE TRAIN STATION, CRACHEE · 11 ·
OF THE CRAZY -5- took THIS PHoto, I'M
50ft - 60ft UP FROM THE STREET. I HAD
to STAND ON THE toES OF MY SNEAKERS
FOR HOURS to do THIS PIECE, BECAUSE
THERE IS ONLY A 4INCH LEdgE. THE PIECE
WAS HUGE BECAUSE I WAS 6ft tALL At
AgE 20 IN THIS PHoto.
                    FEB 12, 1977

"After doin five thousand pieces it's hard to remember them all. This was up there for many years. I had just turned twenty. This was a real challenge for an old guy. All new writers coming up were 14–15 in 1977. I already had a full mustache (Gee Wilikers).
Still havin fun at fifty-one." Blade 2008.

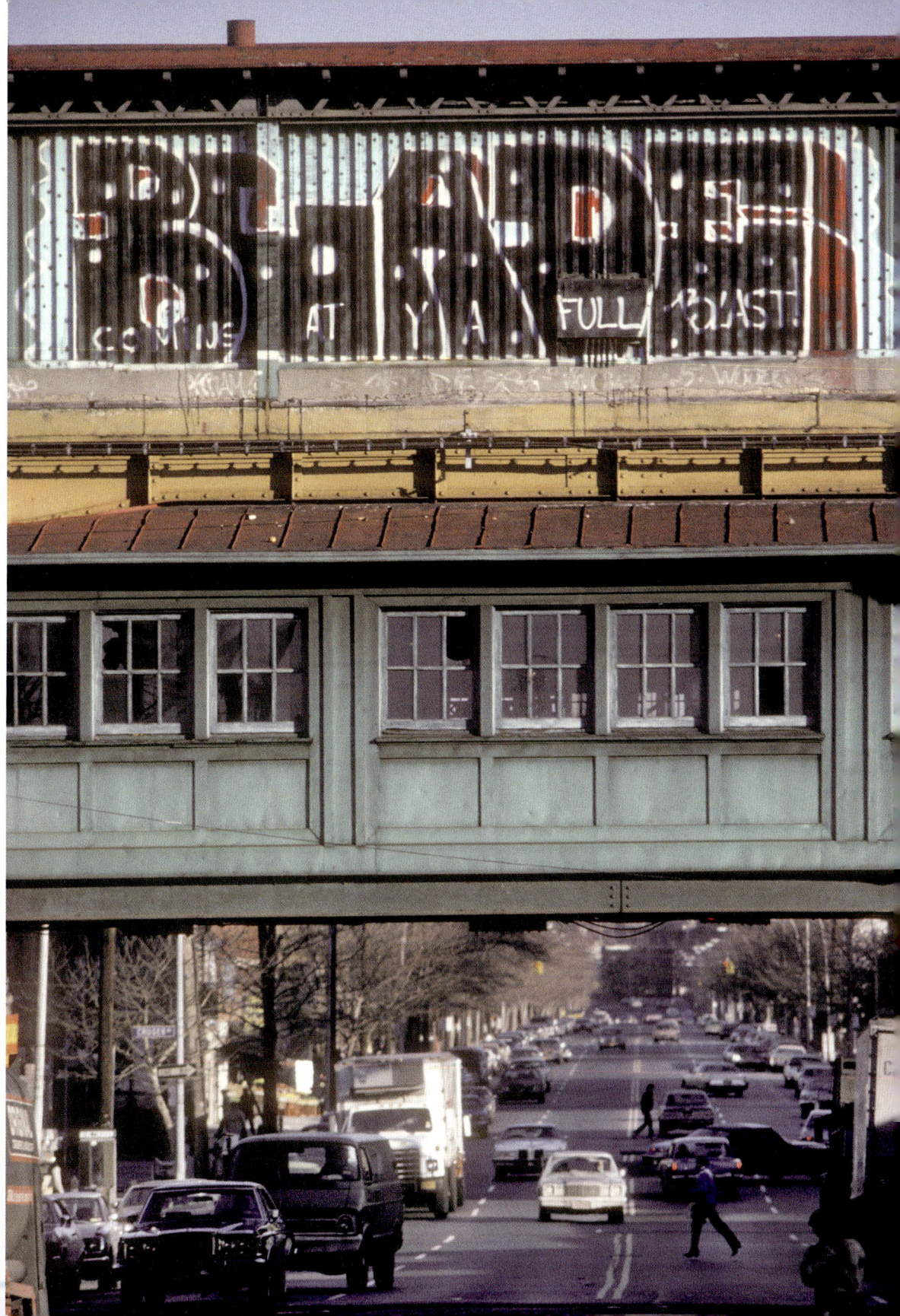

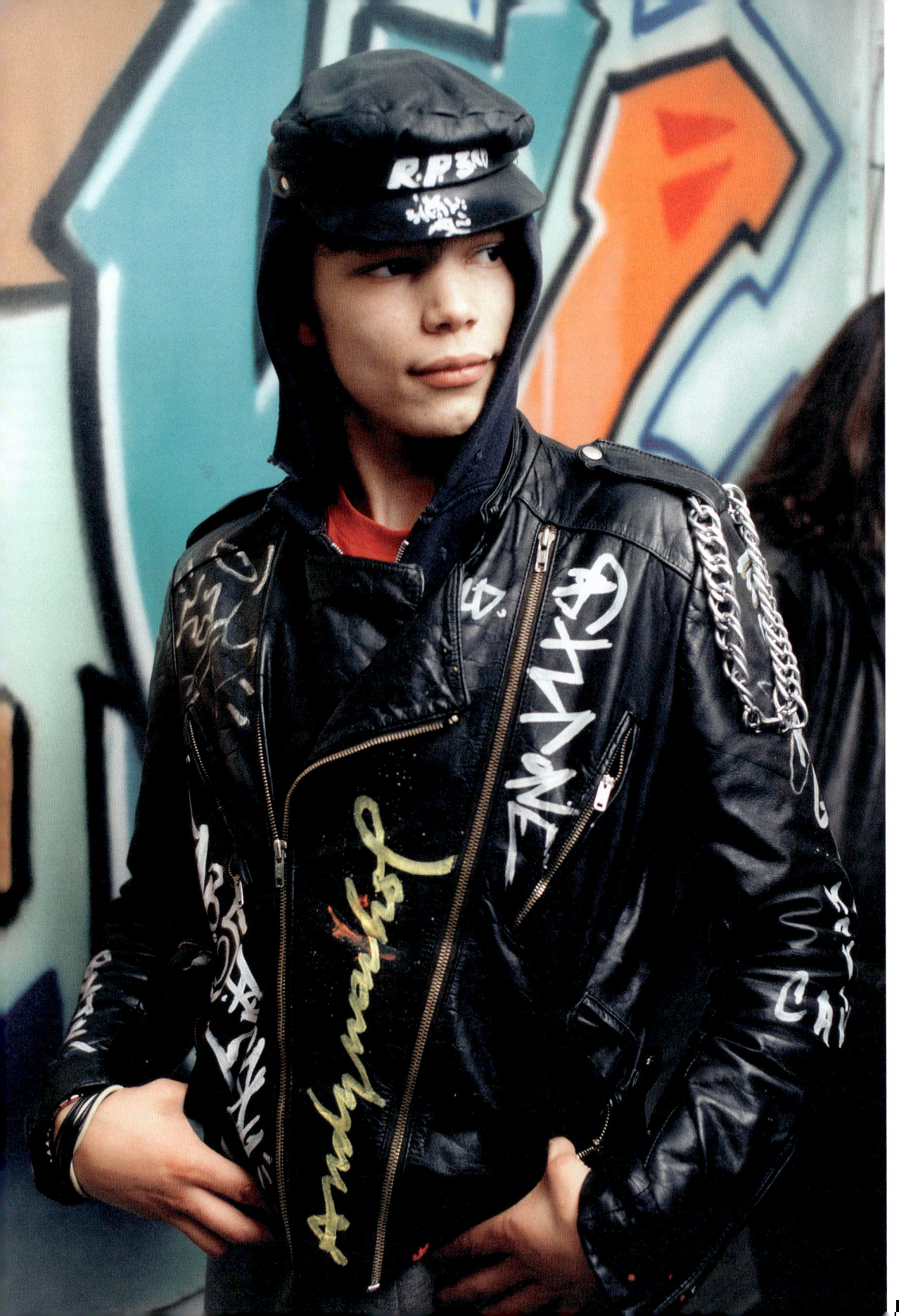

The Fine Art of Tags

Tag styles evolved swiftly on the subway during the 70s as writers pared their names down for quick hits. In public, less was more, but when not in danger of being caught, kids took time to embellish their tags with rich ornamentation in blackbooks or on their personal property.

Around 1980, graffiti connected to the Manhattan art world. Galleries such as Patti Astor's Fun in the East Village and the respected Sidney Janis Gallery on 57th Street encouraged writers to paint canvases and then exhibited them alongside the work of established artists.

Conversely, some artists who had been inspired by graffiti writers, including Kenny Scharf, Keith Haring and Jean-Michel Basquiat, developed their own symbols and painted them on the street. The street art scene owes its existence to this fusion. Graffiti writers led the way in appropriating public space for art.

Legally, tags and street art are both destruction of property. However, these works are experienced differently by the media and the general public. People who aren't familiar with graffiti styles, find tags illegible and ominous. Street art, with its clever graphics and critical commentary about society, is reminiscent of the art seen in museums and galleries and is more easily accepted.

In spite of overwhelming opposition, graffiti has found a place in cities worldwide, its aesthetic reliable and established. Spray painted wildstyle murals have grown to unlimited size, and tags are everywhere. Writers skillfully play with elements derived from the work of thousands of colleagues and other sources from all over the world.

Graffiti writers have created a script so raw and headstrong that it is still perceived as threatening after more than half a century. In doing so, they started the most wide-spread art movement in history. Perhaps graffiti will only be truly appreciated after it has disappeared, but there is no sign that this will happen soon.

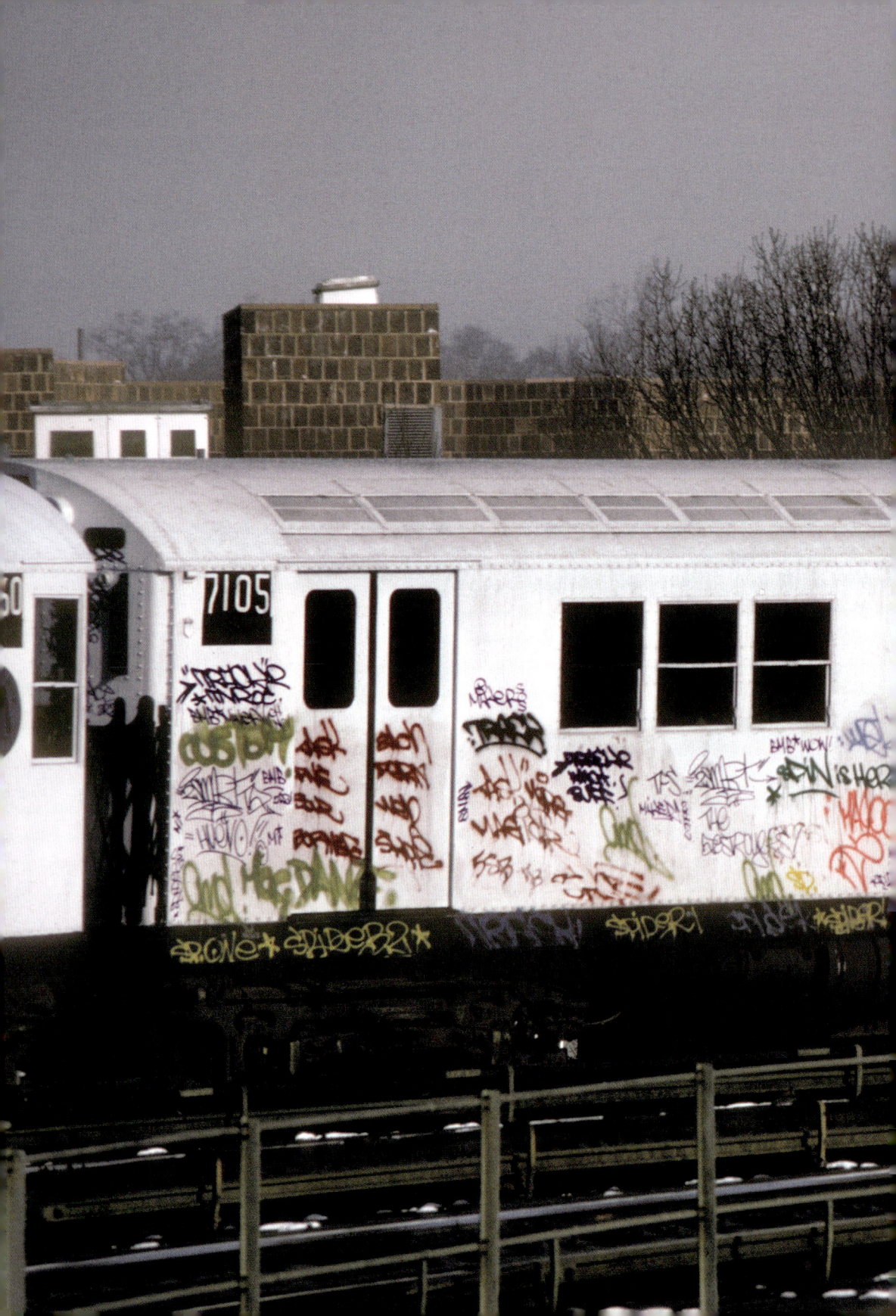

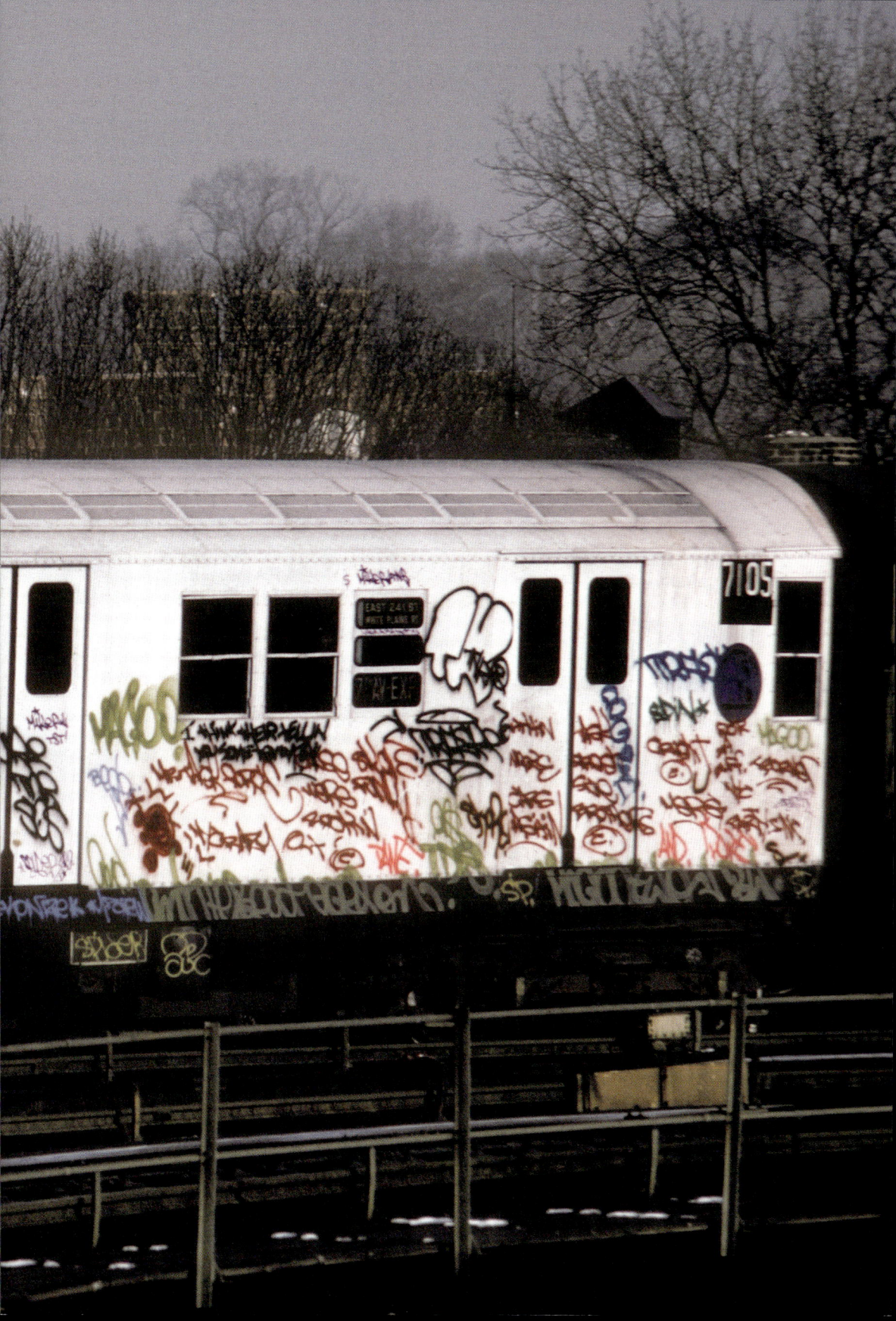

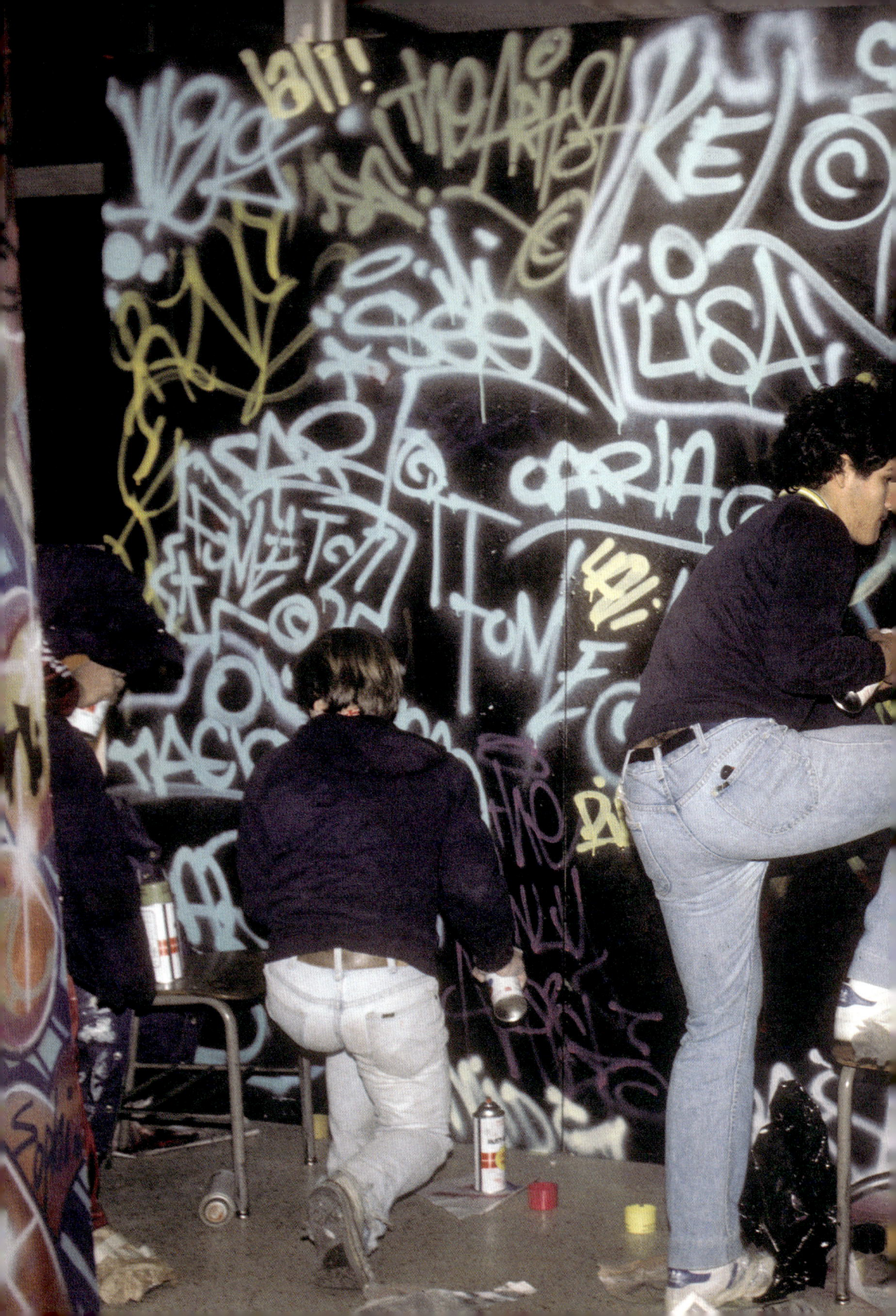

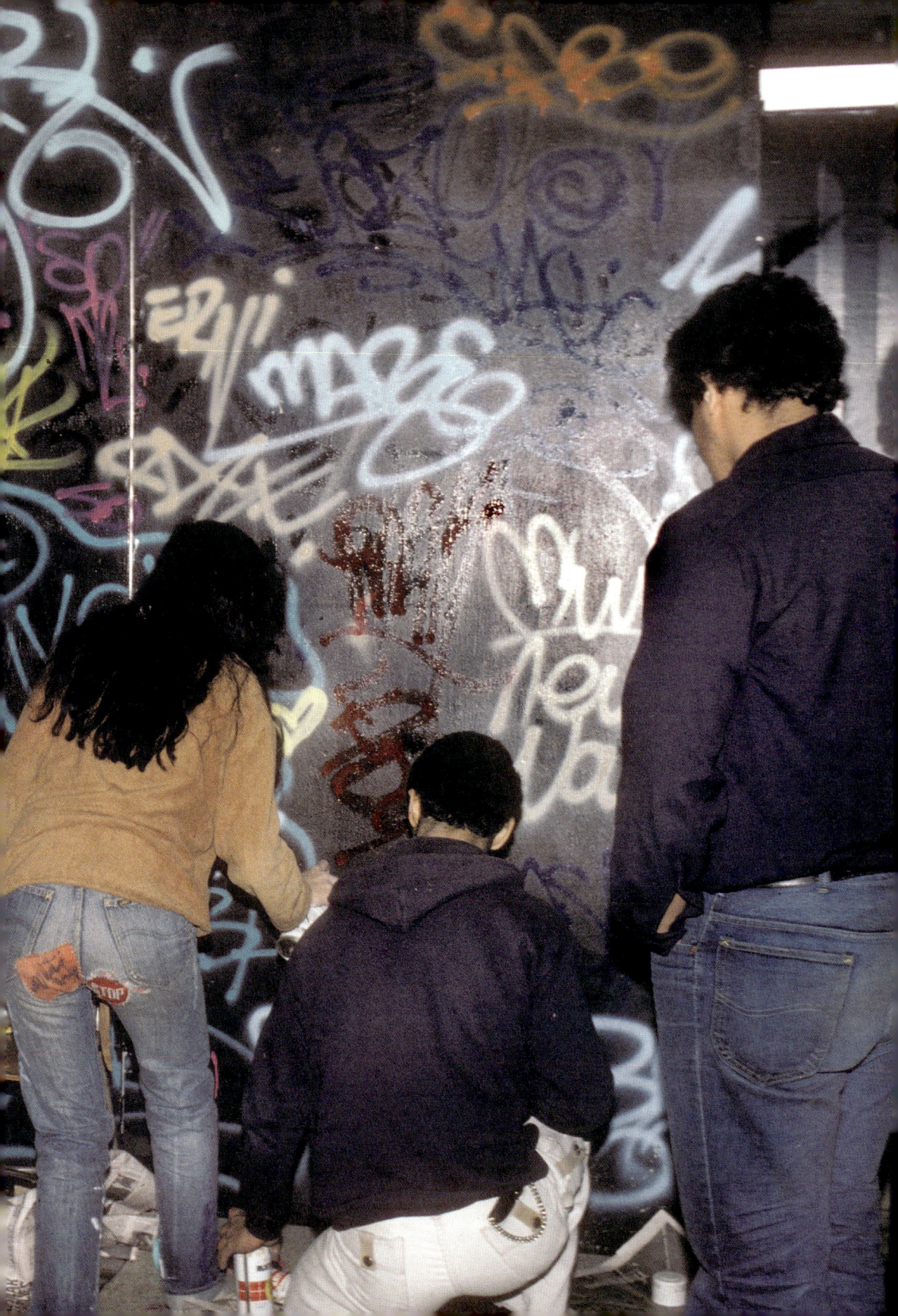

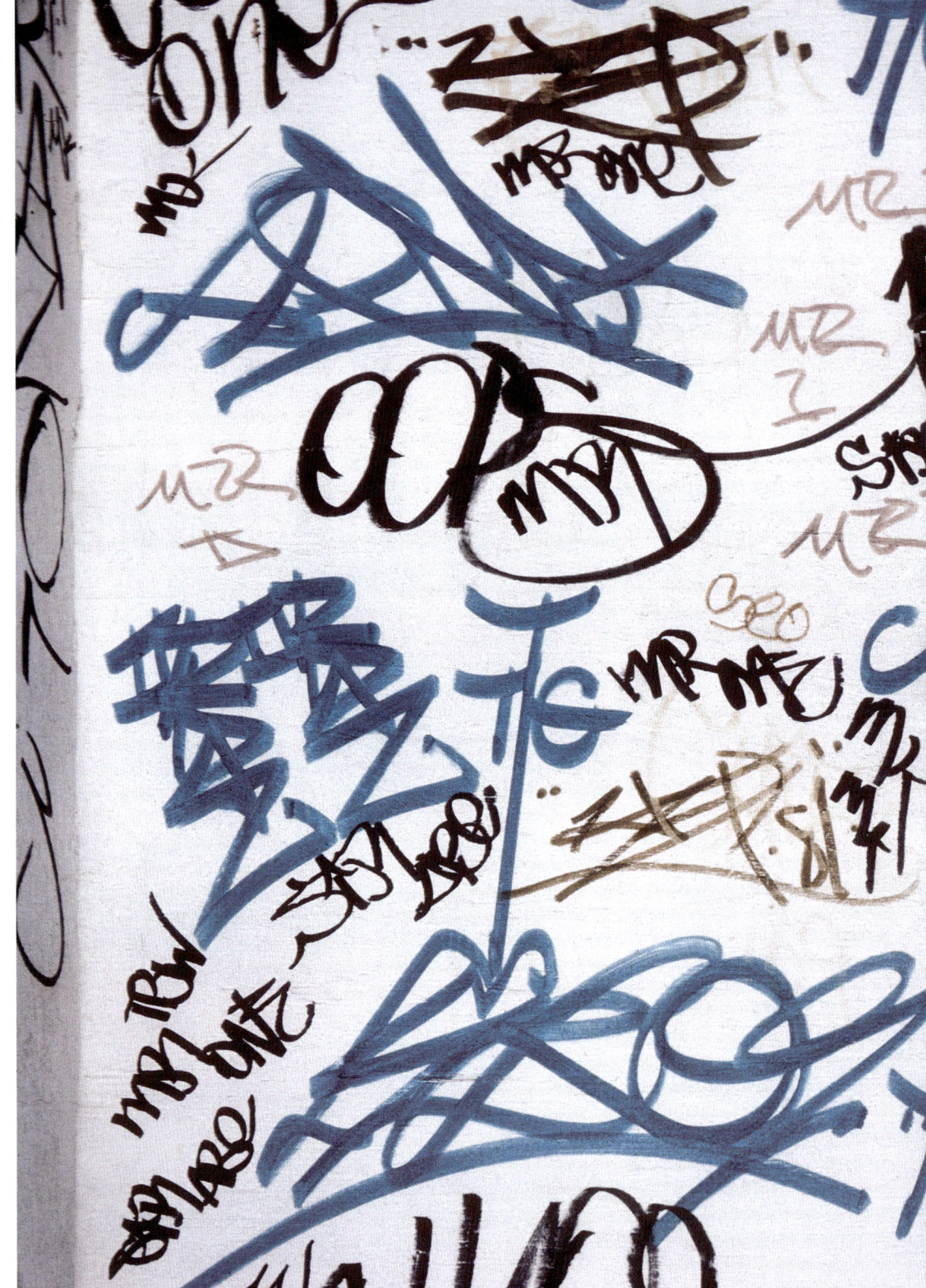

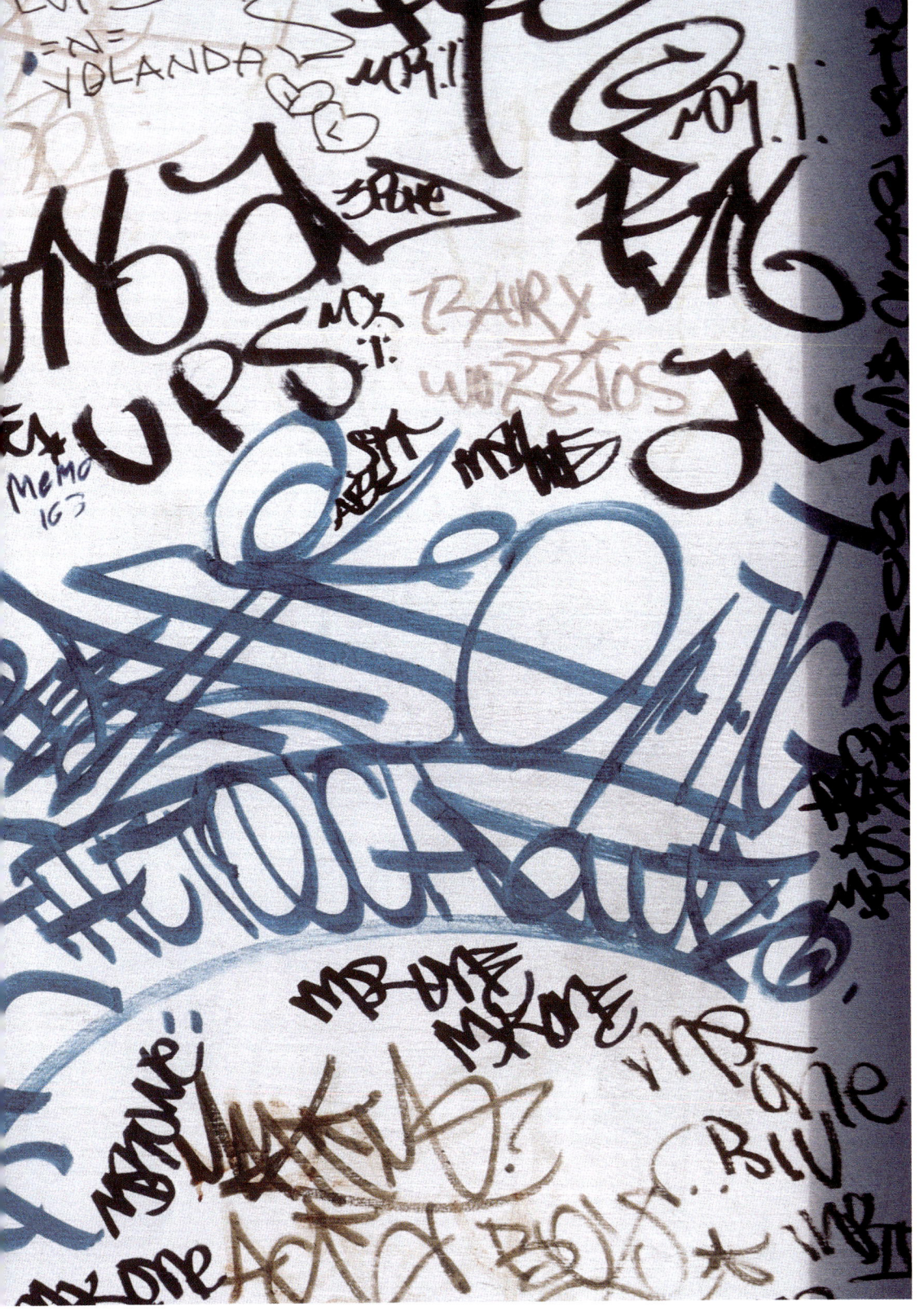

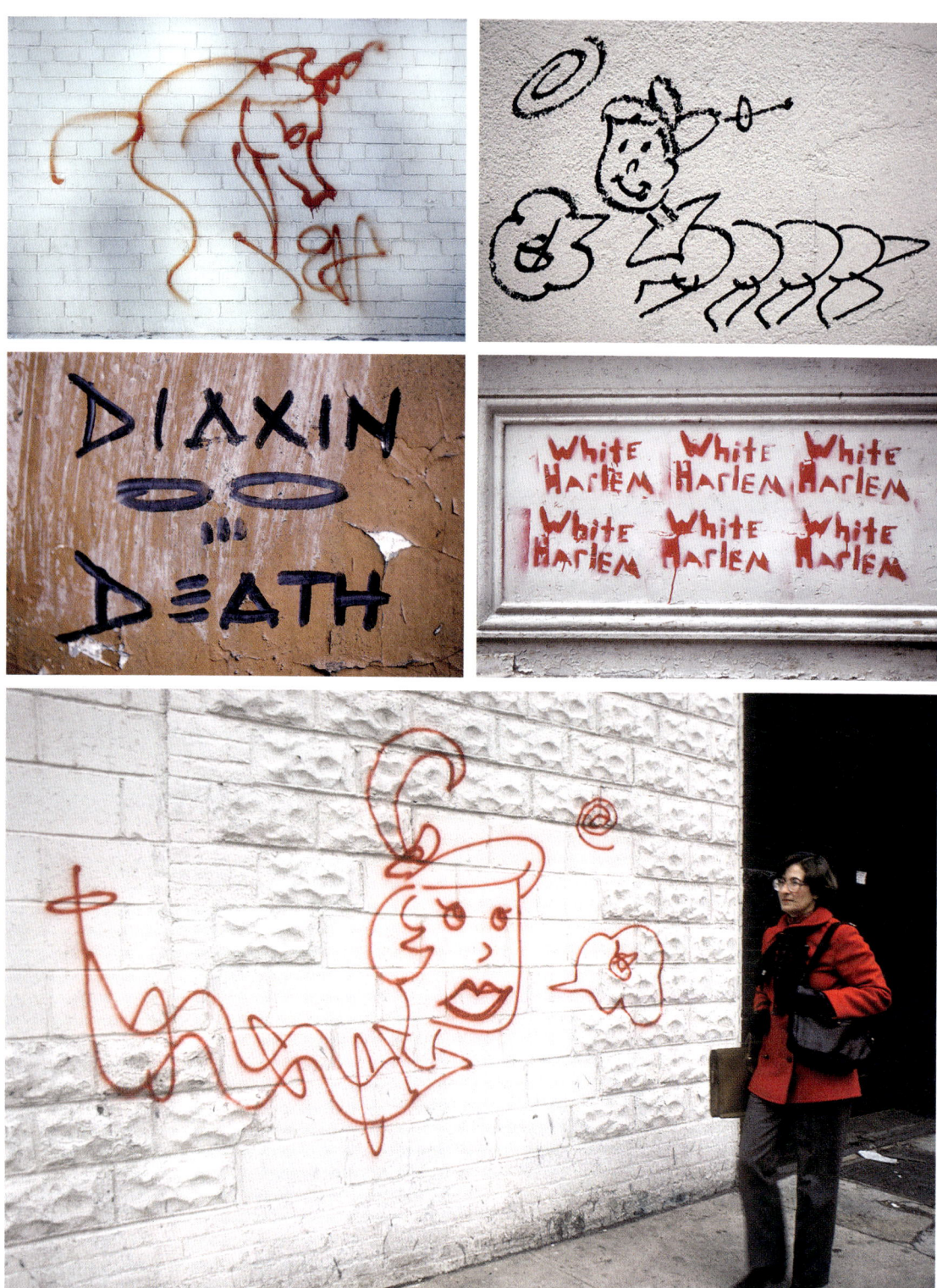

Bottom: A drawing by Kenny Scharf.

The Fine Art of Tags – Street Art

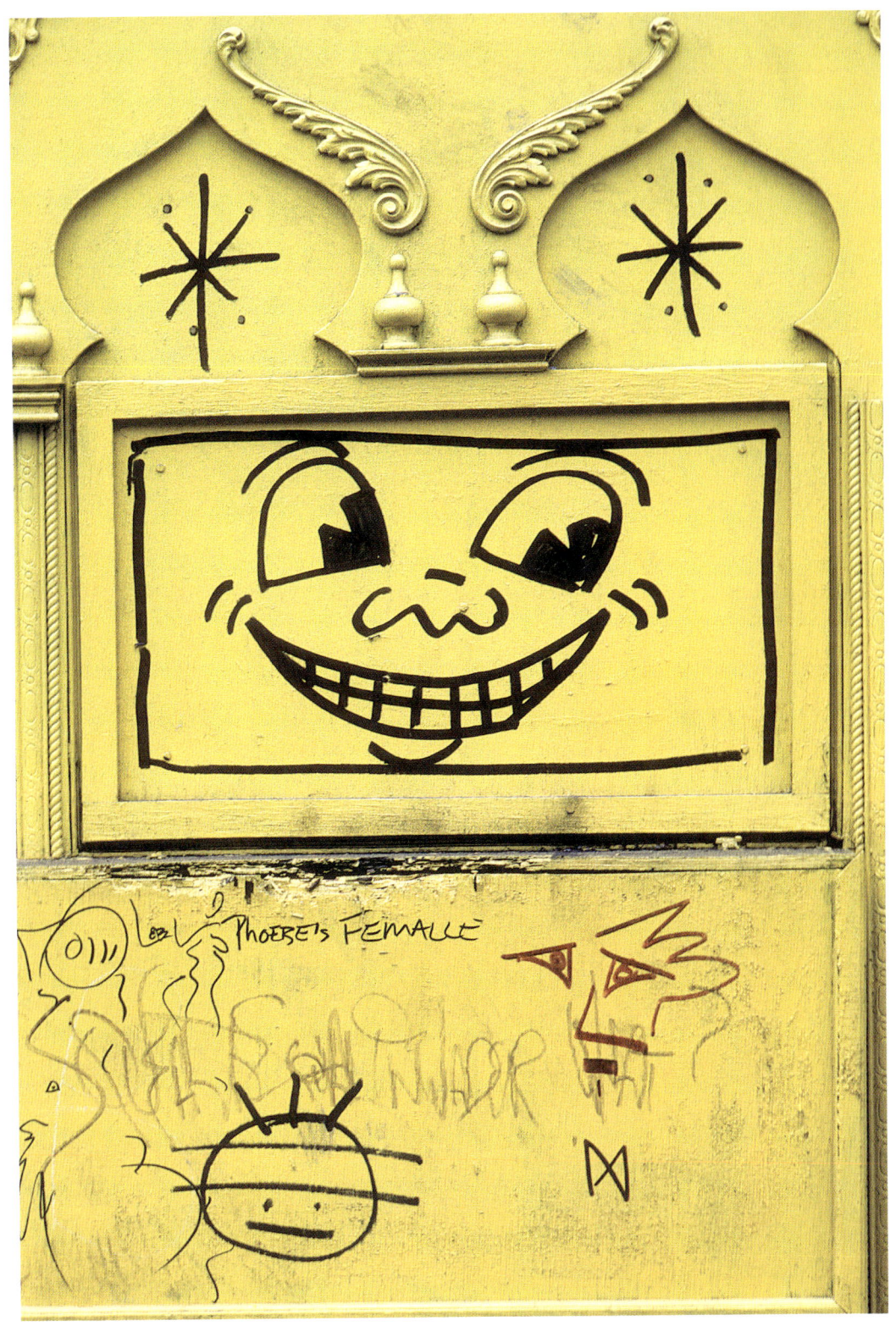

The Fine Art of Tags – Keith Haring

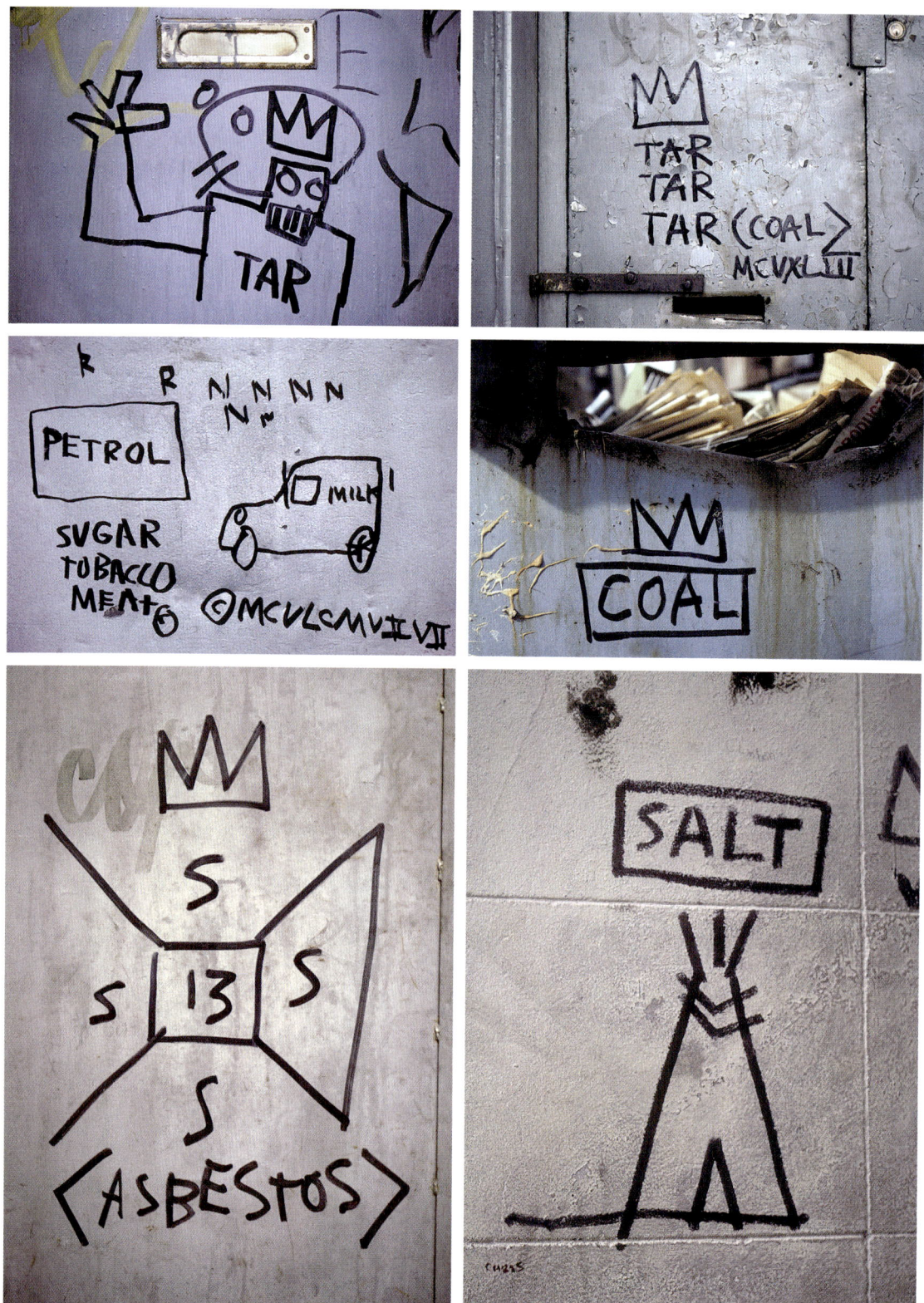

The Fine Art of Tags – Jean-Michel Basquiat

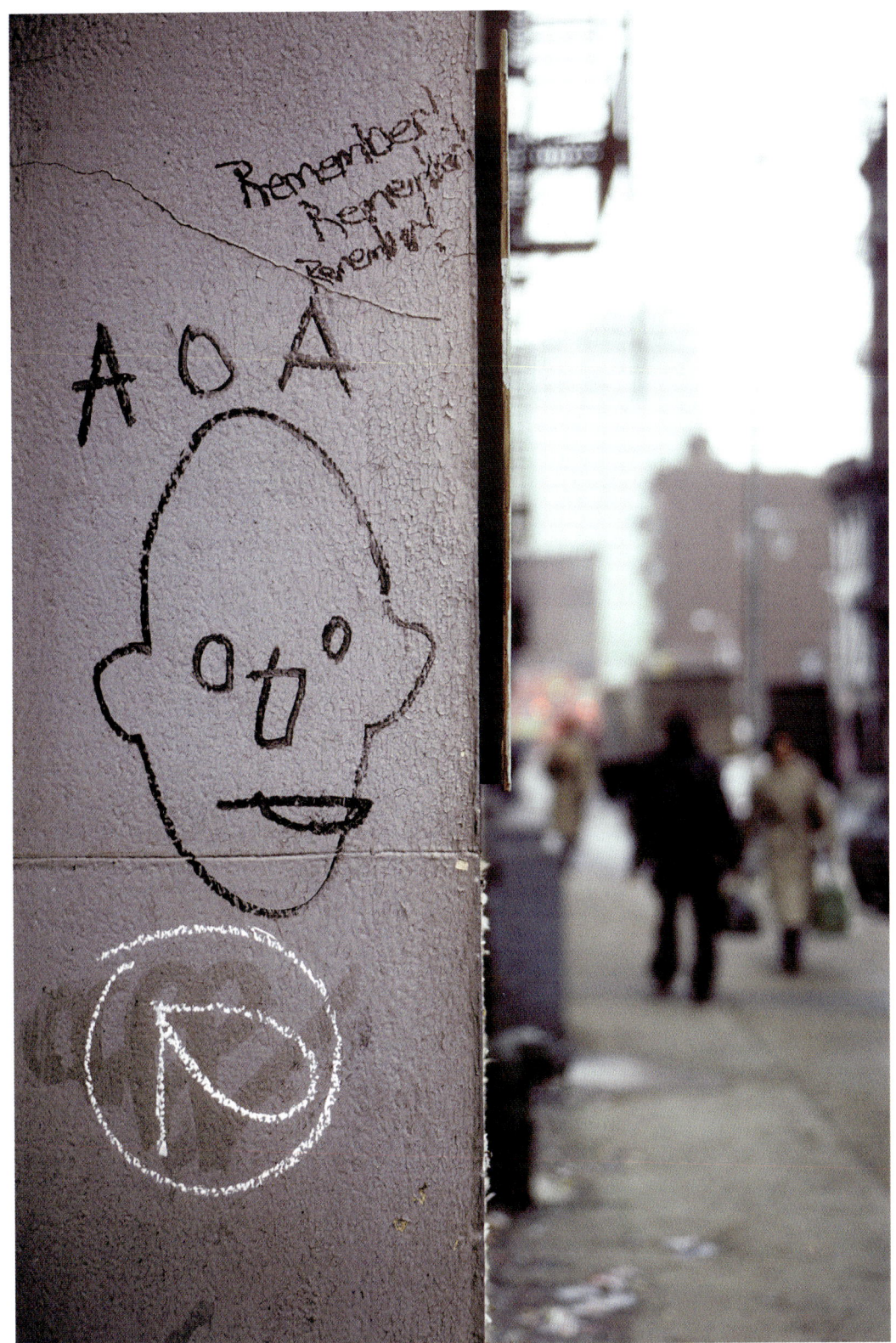

The Fine Art of Tags – Jean-Michel Basquiat

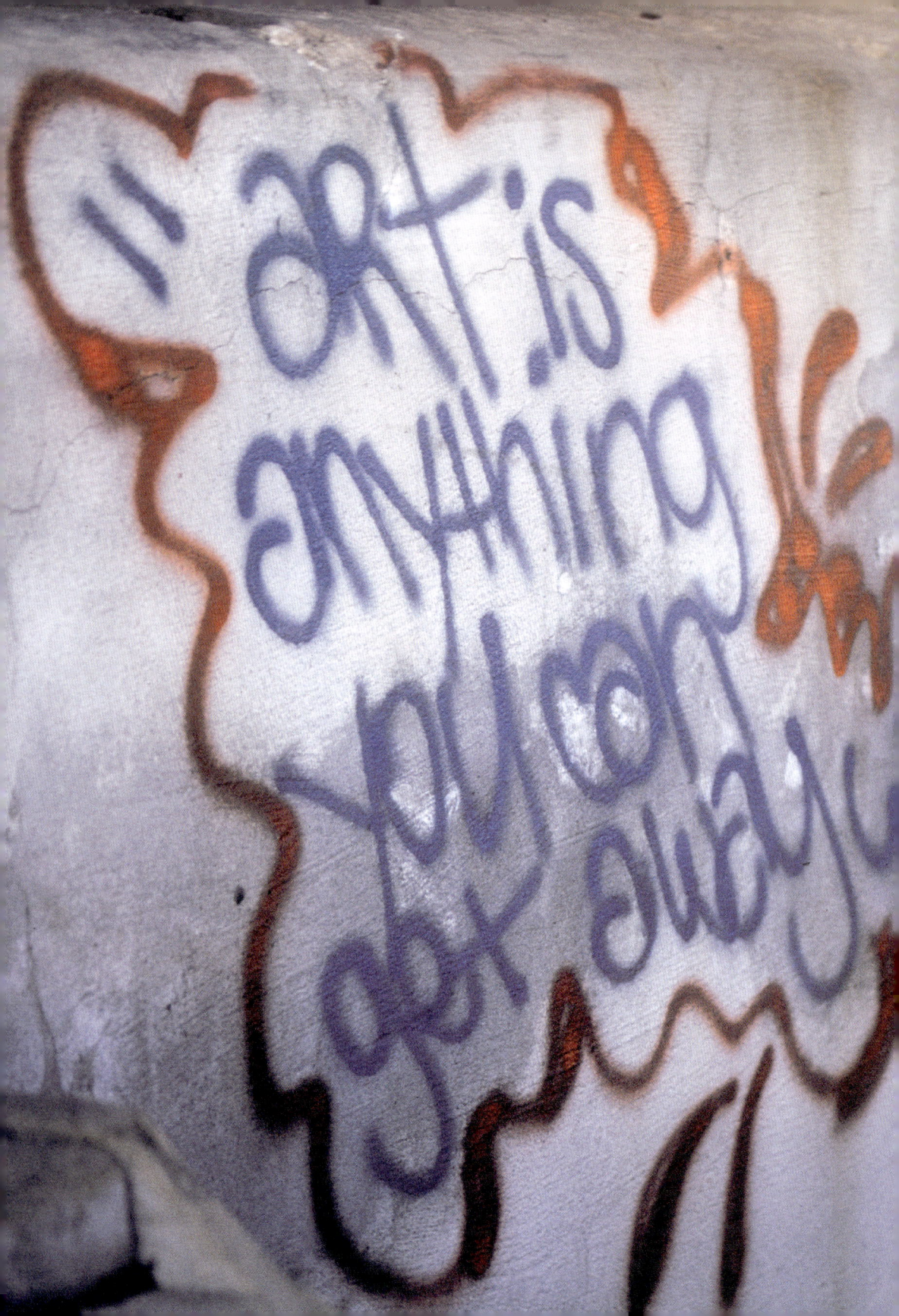

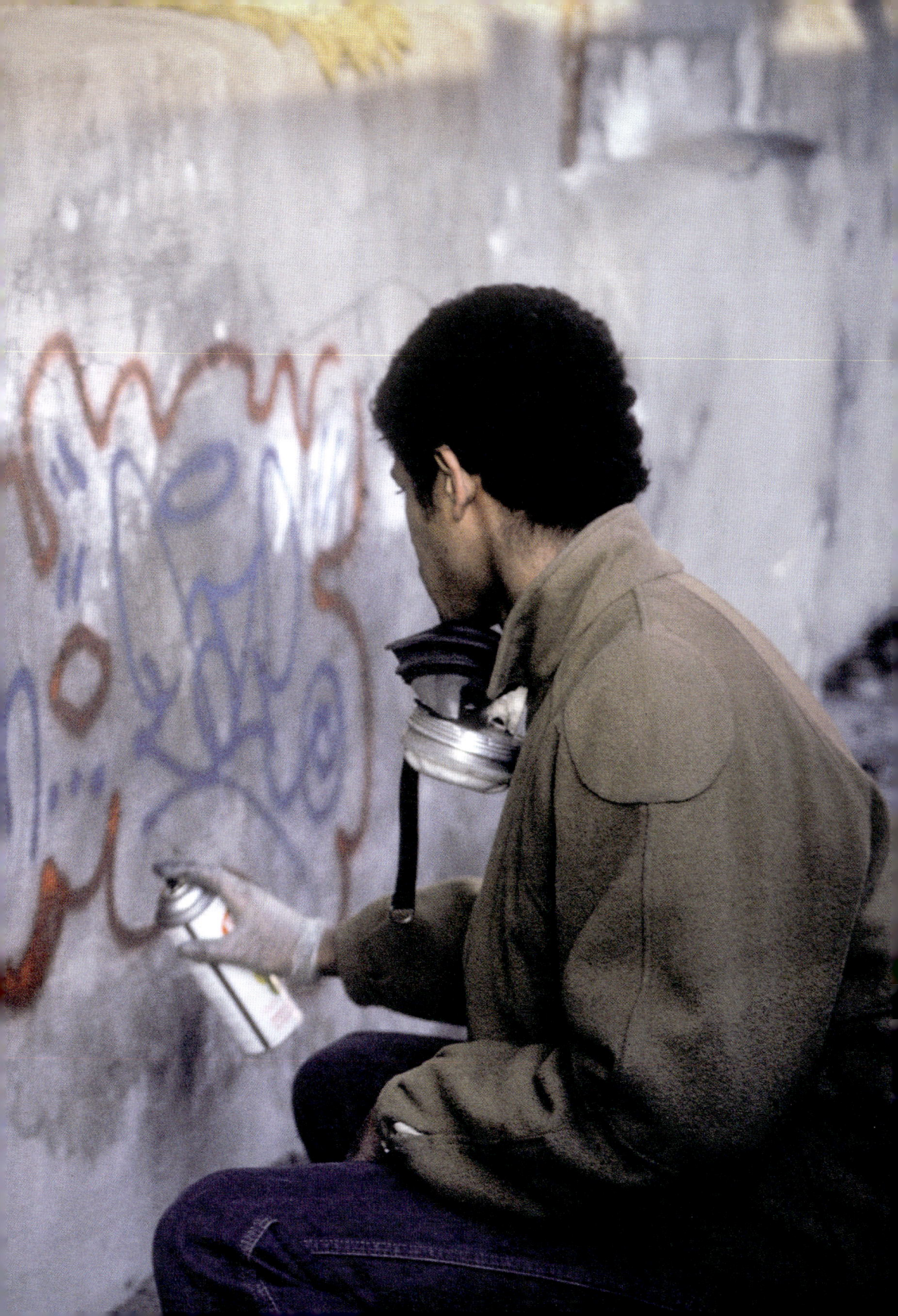

Print Magazine, May/June 1973
Subway Graffiti: The Message from Underground

It started a couple of years ago when undistinguished felt tip scrawls appeared on the seats, walls and doors inside subway cars. Gradually it crept out onto the platforms until the entire wall of the 103rd Street Broadway station was covered with the stuff. By that time the modest felt tips were giving way to a bolder medium – spray can paints – and the scrawls were getting bigger, more colorful and increasingly stylized. Then one morning bleary-eyed strap-hangers did a double-take as familiar trains rumbled into views completely transformed by the drips and swirls of "Stru 5", "Sweet Skip", "King Kool 143" and several hundred of their ego-tripping friends. What may be man's oldest form of graphic expression had mushroomed into New York City's hottest contempotrary art movement: the graffiti explosion.

The critical mass in this explosion is a nucleus of mostly black and Hispanic teenagers from the upper Manhattan ghetto of Washington Heights. Stalking the stations in after-school hours and prowling the yards at night, these kids are engaged in what they regard as more of an in-group sport than an aesthetic exercise. What they're really doing, though, is expropriating the social and economic privileges of those officially sanctioned graffitists, the corporate advertisers. Competing for a captive audience of several million, these unlikely account execs represent the world's most important clients: themselves. The space is free (if they don't get caught), their budgets are the price of a can of spray paint (if they bother to pay for it, which most of them don't) and the product is their own identity.

Eschewing the usual obscenities, political slogans and declarations of eternal affection ("John + Mary 4 ever"), these grassroots media men are plastering the city with their personal logos – name and street number combinations, some of which are as carefully chosen and painstakingly executed as any Madison Avenue blitz. Styles range from small, unembellished monochrome signatures to six-foot-high multicolored bubble letters decorated with stars, stripes, dots and squiggles. Outlining is a popular device because it reinforces shape, and there are also a lot of drip patterns (the "wet" look) and an occasional 3D effect. The layering of colors (frequently pastels) can get pretty complex, and many logos fuse letterform with pictorial motifs like hearts, crowns, arrows, comet tails and stick figures.

A few logos are so elaborate, so highly stylized that they don't read like names at all, but rather like scraps of some exotic calligraphy. There's an informal code of conduct that frowns on writing over someone else's logo (a rule honored as much in the breach as in the observance) and a complicated procedure for selling or handing down names from one graffitist to another.

Although schools and housing projects label graffiti "an act of vandalism" and "a dirty shame", irate citizens suspect that the impulse to write names in public places is related to the wanton murder of mugging victims, and one apparently overwrought newspaper reporter has equated graffitists with "the people who make napalm". (Surely the kids must wish their pastime were so lucrative). Some people consider death by electrocution too good for graffitists; others will settle for chopping off offenders' hands in public. Indeed, the anger and virulence which graffiti have stirred in normally unflappable New Yorkers is weirdly disproportionate to the situation and almost without precedent in recent memory.

The most vociferous protest comes, not surprisingly, from those municipal authorities whose unenviable task it is to halt the outbreak of graffiti on public property. Although some spokesmen will admit, privately, that they kind of like what's happening in the subways, officially they're outraged. Cost of removal, which for the Transit Authority alone was estimated at $500.000 a year ago, is now projected to go as high as $24 million – and that's for erasing only 10 per cent of all graffiti, including what appears on schools and public housing projects as well as subways and buses.

Since the Transit Authority accounts for 27 per cent of this total clean-up bill, that's 500 per cent increase in one year – possibly the fastest escalation in public expenditure since the Vietnam War! Even more appalling is the hopelessness of the task; no sooner is one crop of graffiti removed than another appears in its place. (A newly cleaned surface being an irresistible temptation to any spray can artist.)

Which raises an obvious question: Why is the Transit Authority wasting taxpayers' money in a sudden fit of selfdefeating fastidiousness while more important chores – like repairing inoperative doors, replacing burnt-out lights, securing rickety seats and maintaining or improving directional signs – go perennially unattended?

There's been a lot of speculation about why these kids feel the need to write their names all over the place, but very little analysis of the public hysteria which this phenomenon has provoked. Psychologists diagnose graffiti as "an act of aggression!" and "an attempt by insignificant people to impose their identity on others". Robert Reisner calls it "a twilight means of communication between the anonymous man and the world". But in a vast, impersonal and abrasive city like New York, who doesn't feel "anonymous", "insignificant" or "aggressive" now and then – particularly when trapped in an environment as relentlessly inhuman as the subway? Dank, overcrowded, underlit and terrifying labyrinthian, the New York subway as its best suggests nothing less depressing than a public lavatory; at its worst, it's a vision of purgatory. Is it at all remarkable that so hostile an environment invites vandalism? (Cu-

riously enough, some of the newer "luxury" cars are less heavily marked than the older ones, but this may be because the newer cars don't run on the lines that go into the neighborhoods where most graffitist live.)

Could it be that New Yorkers who enjoy the subway graffiti are simply grateful to discover that somebody – obviously not the TA, but somebody – knows they're there and is taking the trouble to communicate with them? Could it be that those other people who bitterly resent the graffitists recognize, if only subconsciously, that this bunch of "disadvantaged" kids has finally done what they, the good, gray taxpayers, have never had the guts to do: struck back at a system that clearly doesn't care?

O.K., maybe it's not all that great to look at. But can graffiti fairly be condemned in an environment that has long since plumbed the depths of ugliness and neglect? Is being bombarded for 130 blocks by crudely designed hemorrhoid ointment and foot powder ads any less insulting than being told by a free-hand scrawl that "Coco" is alive and well on 144th Street? Isn't that kind of "aggressiveness" preferable to some more violent form of protest?

If nothing else, the subway graffiti are a testimony to the monumental failure of TA officials and their design consultants to make the system legible. Visually, what these kids have created is more coherent than the hodgepodge of dilapidated, poorly located directional signs and paid advertising that makes a trip through the Union Square station a nightmare of wrong turns, missed exits and general disorientation.

True, the graffitists have obliterated most of the system maps, but the maps are practically unreadable anyway.

True, the spraying of paint over car windows makes it difficult for riders to see out. But those windows have always been so dirty, the platform lighting so poor and the platform signs so bad that riders have never been able to know for sure where they are without asking some fellow passenger who has a better view or knows the route by heart. And if people can't figure out where they're going, at least these days they're having more

93

fun getting there. No longer a dreary, non-differentiated routine, the boarding of a subway car is now something of an adventure: yesterday someone may have caught "Hondo", today he's riding "Stay High 149", and tomorrow – who knows?

Whether, when the last logo has been eradicated by super-solvent and the last offender clapped in jail, the writing of graffiti proves to have been a true art form or just the inspiration for another commercial design fad, there's a message in it that city officials and their professional consultants cannot afford to ignore. Somebody up in that ghetto thinks enough of himself to tell the world who he is and how little respect he has for the degraded public environment he's forced to live in.

Imagine what would happen if this message were leaked to all those law-abiding, middle class taxpayers and they, too, suddenly realized that the subway doesn't belong only to TA chief Dr. Ronan and Preparation H – that the subway belongs to them, to the kids up in Washington Heights and to millions of others who are entitled to something a lot better than what they're getting.

Patricia Conway

New York Magazine, March 1973
This Thing Has Gotten Completely Out of Hand

Sometime during the summer of 1970, a guy named Demetrius begins to write his name all over Washington Heights. Only he uses his nickname, which is Taki, and he always adds his street, so the logo reads Taki 183, across stoops and lampposts and handball courts. Always the same legend in the same black scrawl, Taki 183. Pretty soon people are sighting his name like flying saucers, and wondering, what is this squad of Taki-commandos? Rumors begin: it is the surveying crew for a new subway line, or it is a madman quoting stock averages, or it is a street gang so obscure not even Leonard Bernstein knows them, or else it is some kind of arcane religious rite, like when I was a kid and people went around writing "Beware of 1960" on the roofs.

What finally happens is that some guy from the split page of the New York Times tracks Taki down and writes a profile of the dude. And Taki gets to talk about his tricks of the trade, and especially about how great it feels to go around scribbling your name across public property. So that no matter where you are – say, delivering laundry in the farthest reaches of Astoria – there will be your own sanctified scrawl to get you on.

So far it is just the kind of glamor trip New Yorkers are hungering for, a harmless new mania with properly prole undertones. But most people don't realize that Taki is not the only graffitist floating around Washington Heights, and not even the first. There is Eddie 181 and Cay 161 and Julio 204. And these guys are beginning to discover each other's name – that is, Cay might notice Eddie and the two of them might start painting together, sometimes stoned on downs or coke, hit a wall on Audubon Avenue, and maybe a couple of stoops. Pretty soon people in school are noticing, the status mills begin to grind, and suddenly all the

bloods are flashing dry markers the way you might flash a knife. Writing comes to represent a new accessory, like an earring or a car, and everyone begins to cultivate a name for its possibilitites in shape and size. Soon the designs grow ornate, and the technology becomes more complex. Guys travel with five or six widths of marker – Nijis for detail, and Uniwides for broader sweeps. And then, inevitably, spray paint enters the scene, enabling writers to fuzz their names over storefronts and monuments at the flick of a wrist. The paint is a killer to remove. Once marked, the wall is yours.

And then this dude named Top Cat moves to the Heights from Philadelphia and brings with him the Philadelphia style – lean and geometric letters with little platforms. And now the bloods are calling themselves the Broadway Boys and their writing the Elegant style. It becomes an official thing in Washington Heights to write your name somewhere on the intersection of 188th and Audubon, which becomes known as Writers' Corner. Suddenly, kids from all over the city are noticing the Heights, and George Washington High School becomes the school of the seventies (the way Forest Hills High was the school of the sixties). g.w. is where you see High Latin flash – bolero jackets, pimp hats and platform shoes, the overalls cuffed just so. g.w. is where only the teachers look straight, and the kids are engrossed in a kind of bas-couture which must be as fiercely competitive as it seems dazzling to an outsider from Hunts Point.

All this in Washington Heights? You have to understand that the Heights, before the Elegant style, was the city's most anonymous ghetto, filled with miles and miles of endlessly baroque apartment houses, all those powder-stuff bakeries, and dress shops with impossible hems in the window. Washington Heights was so forgotten that hardly anybody except the actual residents realized that the neighborhood was undergoing what the Barrio passed through twenty years ago – a massive Latinization, pouring into the streets a whole generation of kids with the classic urban problem of defending and defining turf. Which makes the Heights an obvious setting for the emergence of graffiti, since now, here is an opportunity to claim your neighborhood and your street, not the way kids in the fifties did it, gang against gang, but in true seventies style: self-reliant – you are responsible for spreading your name, and yours alone.

Soon kids all over the city are discovering the power of ubiquity which graffiti offers, and an astute observer can tell a writer's race and neighborhood from his style. Guys from the Bronx draw little clouds around their names, and favor plump, curvaceous lettering. Out in Brooklyn, they draw ornate comet-tails around lettering which is so abstract as to appear indecipherable. Blacks adopt hip names like Nova, Lazar, Spin, and Nod; or African day-names like Cudjoe, Cuffy, Kwakoe. Puerto Ricans stick to their given names or else choose nicknames which are either Spanglish or hyper-American (Stitch, Snake, Cano, The Malo). Some names are chosen for their sheer mystique. Hitler ii picked his name without knowing who his predecessor was.

By now there are formal groups, like WAR (for Writers Already Respected), and the code of the gang begins to influence even as individual an activity as writing. It is unethical to cover anyone else's name. Logos may be sold or handed down, but Roman numerals must be added to those names which originated elsewhere, and sometimes the process becomes exceedingly elaborate, so that you wonder how it was that Rican XLIV determined his identity.

A writer's life-style emerges, with its own distinctive slang. To steal something is to invent it. ("I invented a can of paint last night"). Any policeman, but especially a transit cop, is called a narco. A writer labels his inferiors toy ("He's a toy writer", "T.A.s are toy cops"). To write on anything is to hit it. A subway car is a wagon.

Soon there are writer's hangouts all over the city. During the day there is a coffee shop on Jerome Avenue across DeWitt Clinton High. Late at night there are these soda-clubs in midtown – most of them sequestered between office buildings and card shops – where young Latinos go to get out of the neighborhood and dance. Certain stations such as the abandoned platform at 91st Street on the Broadway IRT, are as sacred as Writers' Corner. Reputations are made and lost on these walls. There are legendary writers like Phase 2 (who is widely credited with introducing the Bronx "bubble" style at Clinton High) and Stay High 149, who adorns his name with a stick figure smoking a joint. These people are spoken of in the kind of reverentist hush once reserved for Che Guevara and Willie Colón. Was it Phase 2 who used to work in white gloves so that only the hands were visible? How did Jee and Mike 171 manage to write their names on jet planes in Puerto Rico?

Finally, a younger generation of writers emerges – kids who are fourteen to seventeen, too young for gangs, and too healthy for junk. These kids regard Taki with no little disdain (he was always wearing sandals, he had no flash, he only wrote in black). They are unwilling to settle for monuments and walls. They want the maximum yield in visibility. And so, finally, some young geniuses realize that the very source of all mobility in this town, the one place where everybody you are ever going to meet on the street will have to see your name, is the subway. The jive IRT.

It seems harmless enough at first. Couple of kids from the Heights sneak down into the yards at night, stalking the tracks like the Dead End Kids in their overalls and polo shirts, wearing Mother's rubber gloves and baggy Army fatigue jackets to hide the spray paint – Red Devil and Rust-oleum being the preferred brands – and each can specially fitted with the wider nozzle from spray starch or Scotchgard, so the flow is fast and thick. Some dude has cribbed a set of keys from a conductor, so they can open any door, turn on the lights, blow the horns. And the wagons are sitting there like silent whales, and the kids set about altering the flesh forever, bodies moving up and down like action painters, deft, stealthy, until the whole thing, inside and out, begins to resemble the waves of someone's broken color TV. And in the morning, when the wagons are put into operation, they'll whiz down Broadway past the astonished eyes of maybe 100.000 dank souls, all of whom will have been subjected to the ace experience of meeting Snake 1 or Stitch or Turok 161 or Trik as they wish to be met.

Suddenly this thing has gotten completely out of hand. The Krylon conspiracy is upon us, and no reporter from the split pages of The Times can encompass it, as kids from all over the city take to the tracks. The city fights back. Art suppliers refuse to sell markers and spray paint to kids, but most writers prefer to invent their tools anyway, and a hardy black market in paint and ink keeps them well supplied. The T.A. is helpless against these rhinestone hordes. Of course there is a public show of force. Writers are caught and sometimes punished on the spot by having their faces sprayed. Some are brought to Family Court and forced to scrub stations clean, wearing goggles and gloves. Even Boy Scouts are enlisted in the clean-up attempt. But the T.A. can make no dent in the invasion, and the presence of its toy cops adds just the element of mock-danger these kids crave. There is even an Officer Krupke figure in the person of Officer Schwartz, who is rumored to have busted all the best writers. But the word on Schwartz is that he wears his cop shoes under his jeans, which makes him highly visible to any writer with a sense of style.

Meanwhile whole stations fall to the marker blitz. Trains pull by, buried in a confetti of names and numbers. It becomes a rarity of rarities to find a readable map. Only the advertisements remain untouched (perhaps in a gesture of empathy with certified hype). And there comes that moment when you watch the doors close around a Wall Street executive in a camel's hair coat and cufflinks which glimmer with efficiency, and you know that he is going to have to stand for the next ten minutes staring point-blank into the wobbly green

T drawn freehand the night before by some balmy teenager in the yard.

About now you're wondering why someone doesn't come along and organize these kids – all the talent applied to some constructive purpose, as the Junior League ladies might say. Well, there is Hugo Martinez, a 22-year-old sociology student at City College. On October of 1972, Martinez forms the United Graffiti Artists along with the top twelve writers from Washington Heights. Each writer agrees to retire from subway decor in exchange for membership privileges. They meet in Martinez's apartment near the Soldiers and Sailors Monument (which many writers call Grant's Tomb). There, they write on oaktag and canvas, elaborate versions of the designs they used to draw in the subways. Martinez has given these kids the idea that they can build something tangible for themselves – like, say, a career in the arts.

First, he persuades the art department at City College to stage an exhibition of graffiti. Next, he arranges for the U.G.A. to design backdrops for Twyla Tharp's ballet, *Deuce Coupe*, at the Joffrey, six or seven dudes dressed in platforms and jeans spray away on stage while the performance takes place. The dance is an immense success – the hit of the season, actually – and suddenly, media men want to tap the source of this stylistic coup. The boys become accustomed to attention, and the most photogenic begin to preen at the drop of a flashcube. Ray-B 954, who is fourteen and lives in Hunts Point, has been on four channels in the past three months. He is now acting as a business manager for the group, taking commissions for canvases and auto décor. Call it the New Realism. For a hundred bucks you can buy a U.G.A. original and choose the colors yourself. Would Ivan Karp stand for that?

Meanwhile, the rush is on. Hugo is negotiating with the New York Cultural Center for a major graffiti show in June. A lady up in Riverdale wants to have the U.G.A. do her dining room wall. People are talking about … graffiti Christmas cards, ad copy, window dressing (already there is a boutique on the Concourse called Taki 183). Suddenly this thing is bigger than Throat. The

97

U.G.A. is looking for a studio in Washington Heights and hustling funds for its projects. Hugo's selling point in graphic: the only way to get the graffiti off the subway is to elevate them into art.

Maybe the whole thing will end up as a series of greeting cards featuring piquant couplets from old-time rock 'n' roll, but at least the exploitation is mutual. What Hugo has done is to take a group of young street people and turn them into working commercial artists. They seem sensible enough to regard their acceptance with skepticism, and nobody is counting on a career as Writer-in-Residence at the School of Visual Arts. It is still far more prestigious to see your name on the IRT than on the Joffrey Playbill, and it's far more glamorous to meet the real Phase 2, after seeing his name on so many walls, than to meet the real Twyla Tharp.

Actually, these kids all turn out to be rather ordinary fourteen- or fifteen-year olds. There is Charmin 65 – née Virgin 1 – the only woman who is not regarded as a toy writer (since she hit the Statue of Liberty last summer). And there is Mike 171, one of two Europeans in the group, who speaks with a Puerto Rican slur. And Co-Co 144, very short and thin, with comb-black hair, scuffed platform shoes, and the requisite jeans, cuffed and worn with the top snap open so that he is constantly checking out his fly.

Co-Co lives with his parents and his wife Tiny, who also writes. He is sixteen, she is fifteen. They share a tiny room, her dolls spread out across his bureau, a large plastic Snoopy hanging on the wall. Co-Co's parents seem to love him deeply, and they sit politely in the kitchen while he gives interviews. There is no disapproval shown toward Co-Co's writing; rather, they seem to recognize it as an integral part of his personal style, and they show me his oaktag paintings the way my parents used to show my poems to company.

One of these things that strike you about these kids is how good they look – so different from the ghetto junkie image. Though their experiences with drugs vary widely, none of these kids seem dominated by the Big Nod. They are healthy-looking and athletic. At home, their writing is often displayed along with trophies and medals, in the center of the household, on top of the TV.

The writers themselves seem to regard writing graffiti as though it were a sport rather than an art. It is something men do together in teams, something which requires meticulous attention to form, mastery of technology, and evasion of hostile forces, represented by the T.A. Some spirit of the hunting party is involved in all of these groups, and when they speak of their days in the yards together, you begin to glimpse something of the masculine romance which graffiti can provide.

It may just be that the kids who write graffiti are the healthiest and most assertive people in their neighborhoods. Each of these people has to "invent" his life – his language, his culture are lifted, remodeled and transformed. In that ferocious application of energy to style lies the source of all flash, and the reason why immigrant groups exert such a powerful impact on popular taste. Style involves conflict, the strain of races, classes, ages, and sexes pitted against each other in the arenas of clothing and music and slang. For a long time I wondered how lower-class kids in this city were going to enter the fray. And then I began to look closely at the subway writers, at their use of color and design, at the way they dressed, putting chunks of other people's fashions together in a way that clashed, but coherently I began to think about how coherent the subways look these days, as though each writer were working within a pattern which was consistent with his larger sense of how things ought to look. And I began to feel that the most significant thing about graffiti was not their destructiveness but their cohesion, bringing together a whole generation of lower-class kids in an experience which is affirmative and delinquent at the same time.

In that sense, the graffiti movement is a lot like rock 'n' roll in its pre-enlightened phase. To me, it announ-ces the first genuine teenage street culture since the fifties. Not another season of imitation-psychedelia, but a fiercer, hotter style, much closer to the spirit of *West Side Story* than *Easy Rider*. If all this begins to seem as compelling to middle-class kids as the J.D. style did twenty years ago, then we are in for some inventive times.

Richard Goldstein

Harper's Magazine June 1975
The Curse of Commercial Cursive
And Other Calligraphic Curiosities

One of the curious by-products of our automated culture is the value people place on "communication". By this word we generally mean the process of getting information from one place (or person) to another. We now can do this in more different ways using more different kinds of machines than ever before. The written word in particular has been gobbled up by "communication", and most of the written words we see are made by machines. Occasionaly one gets a handwritten postcard or letter, but most words come in typewritten or printed forms that are easy to process, reproduce, and file – to serve as units in the process of data transfer.

Before Gutenberg began all this by inventing movable types in about 1437, and in countries where this invention did not catch on so quickly, the written word served purposes other than communication. In particular, the act of writing has been used as a form of artistic expression.

Writing done for the sake of expression as well as communication is called calligraphy, and in China, Japan, and much of the Middle East it enjoys a status equivalent to that of painting in the West. In an essay called "The Enjoyment of Culture", Lin Yu-tang, the great Chinese philologist, gives an idea of how much written forms can express:

"In painting and calligraphy, particularly the latter, we are able to see a whole category of aesthetic qualities of different types of beauty, and no one will be able to separate the beauty of the finished product and the beauty of the artist's own soul. There may be beauty of whimsically and waywardness, beauty of rugged strength, beauty of massive power, beauty of spiritual freedom, beauity of courage and dash, beauty of romantic charm, beauty of restraint, beauty of soft gracefulness, beauty of austerity, beauty of simplicity and 'stupidity', beauty of mere regularity, beauty of swiftness, and sometimes even the beauty of afflicted ugliness. There is only one form of beauty that is impossible because it does not exist, and that is the beauty of strenuousness or of the strenuous life."

Calligraphy in Europe had a similar range of expressive power until Gutenberg put nearly all the scribes out of business with his wonderful device. Then writing began to degenerate into its present status: a utilitarian skill, still necessary enough that we teach our children how to do it, but mostly used when typing is impractical. If someone were to invent a really efficient voicewriter, which printed words as one spoke into it, we'd probably scratch penmanship off school curriculums altogether.

But maybe not. Culture is full of surprises and one of the most recent is the sudden burst of interest in calligraphy. Just as communication seems on the verge of stamping out handwriting once and for all, throngs of people are discovering that they like to write for the sake of writing. It's fun.

The two most aggressive forms of this renaissance stand at opposite ends of the respectability scale. On one hand, there is a massive resurgence of interest in formal calligraphy, notably the kind of writing called italic, which looks like this:

The quick brown fox jumps over the lazy dog

On the other hand, there is the Magic Marker boom in New York City. This event has been going on for several years, and has resulted in a new style of writing which now decorates public surfaces all over New York, as well as other cities across the country, and which looks like this:

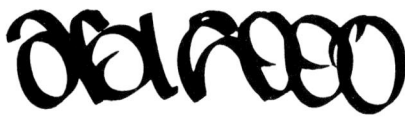

Most people who practice italic writing would not dignify the graffiti in subways with the name "calli-graphy". But if you are not concerned with what's high class, you will notice that the impetus behind the italic revival and the graffiti blight have a lot in common: both come from a discovery of enoyment in the act of writing, and both have elements of rebellion.

"People are reacting against slickness and mass production", Lou Strick said recently of the interest in italic. Mr. Strick is president of the Pentalic Corporation, the only company that handles calligraphic supplies exclusively. You can order pens, ink, paper, and letter-form books from Pentalic, 132 West Twenty-second Street, New York, NY 10011.

Pentalic is doing very well these days. "I've been in this business eleven years now", said Mr. Strick, "and the rate of increase in our sales has doubled and tripled in that time. It's especially shot up in the last couple of years. The new Whole Earth Epilog has a whole page devoted to calligraphy, and our orders are increasing all over the country. I would say it is part of the general interest in crafts going on now. If someone is just casting around for a craft, nothing is more practical or rewarding. There is nothing artificial about calligraphy – from the moment you become more sensitive to your own writing you can begin to derive a great deal of pleasure from it. And you can practice whenever you write."

Besides Pentalic's sales figures, there are other symptoms of the growing interest. A major one is the Calligraphy Workshop, which opened about a year ago in Manhattan and is the first school in the country devoted exclusively to the art. It attracts many professional calligraphers, who mainly do such work as lettering for book jackets, as well as lots of ordinary folk who just want to learn for their own enjoyment. Most of its classes teach italic, and are overenrolled within days of their announcement.

People who live outside New York can learn italic very well on their own, using an instruction manual like *Italic Calligraphy and Handwriting*, by Lloyd J. Reynolds. Pentalic first published this volume in 1969, and has since sold over 40.000 copies. The other necessary equipment is paper, and a pen with a broad flat nib, which automatically produces the thick and thin lines that make italic look so spiffy. Osmirod used to be the classic italic pen, but Mr. Strick now recommends a British pen called Platignum.

Although you can learn italic fairly easily at any age, the most sensible time to learn would be as a child, before you have to unlearn the "commercial cursive" that is now taught in all American schools. Real calli-graphers detest commercial cursive, because it is ugly, and most kids don't like it very much either, but they have no idea that other styles of writing exist. Experiments show that children can write legible italic faster than legible cursive. Lloyd Reynolds, who wrote Pentalic's best-seller, teaches calligraphy at Reed College in Portland, Oregon, and he has recently scored the calligraphy coup of the decade by getting the State of Oregon to adopt italic as an alternative system of writing in its public schools. As teachers begin to learn the new styles, and more and more schools make the switch, one can foresee the day when everyone in Ore-gon writes like a Renaissance scribe.

Children in New York City, no more satisfied with commercial cursive than their West Coast contemporaries, have taken matters into their own hands. As the ubiquitous graffiti artist Taki 183 discovered several years ago, a felt-tipped marker with a broad flat nib produces satisfying thicks and thins when used for writing. In fact, a felt marker is just as good for writing italic as a Platignum pen, although it requires a larger writing surface – something like the nice smooth enamel interior of a subway car. The italic style was unknown to Taki and his many disciples, but like all calligraphers they discoverd that commercial cursive looks absurd written with a thick-and-thin line, and they simply experimented. The result is the relatively consistent script known as Broadway which now festoons the subway cars that run under Broadway and other avenues in New York. It looks like this:

This is a group signature by The Kools Inc., and contains the writing of at least three different people: Piece 2, Cash 5, and Solo 1.

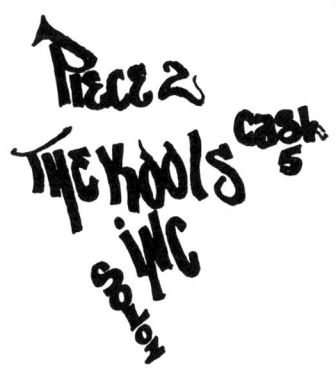

While this style of writing may seem almost illegible to the eye that is used to printed letter forms, you have to remember that this is not writing meant to "communicate" but to express the beauty of flamboyance and power – as in this example:

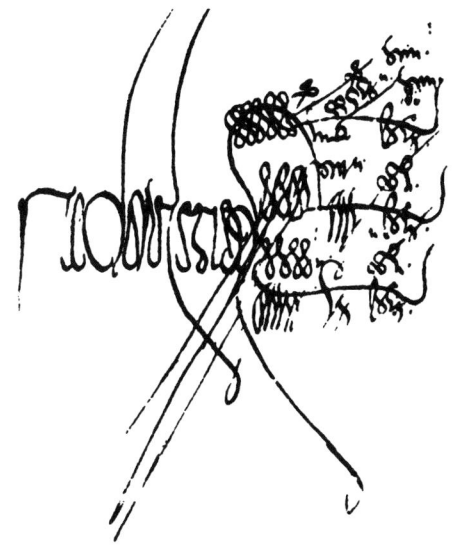

This one does not come from the subway but from an eighth-century charter of Charles the Great. The signature is that of Rado.

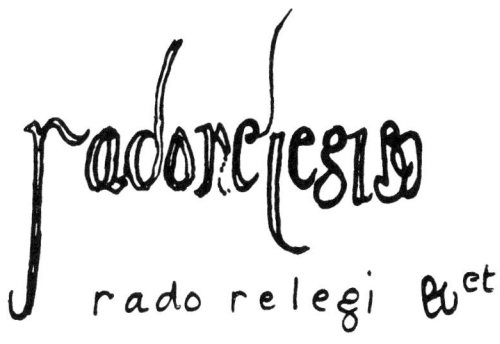

rado relegi et

Essays – The Curse of Commercial Cursive And Other Calligraphic Curiosities

Rado wrote in a style called Merovingian, which flourished 1.200 years before the advent of Broadway, but which has a number of similar characteristics. Both use something of a back-hand slant, and both favor extreme verticals.

Decoded, they look like this:

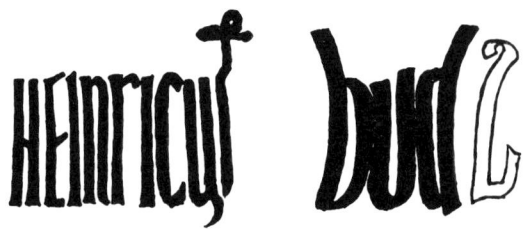

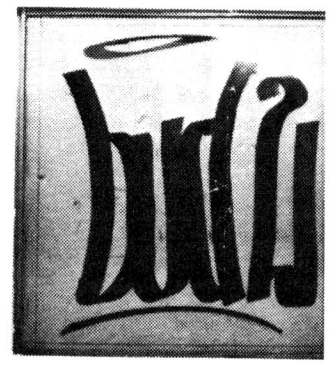

Although a whole millennium separates the signatures of Bud 2 and Heinricus (1, presumably), the most obvious difference is not in the letter forms, but in the fact that one costs thousands of dollars to buy and the other costs thousands of dollars to erase.

David McClelland

To the left: Eleventh century, charter of Emperor Henry IV. Right: Twentieth century, Lexington Avenue subway, New York City.

Village Voice 1982
New Wave Graffiti

Maybe it's the peculiar despertation of graffiti wars — with crews battling over bits of underground turf – or maybe the spectre of guard dogs in the transit yards; but the scourge of the subways is definitely moving aboveground. With its change of venue, a change in sensibility is in the wind, as graffiti writers move from mammoth swaths of color to something more closely resembling New Wave art, or as it's sometimes called, Visual Punk.

In Soho and Tribeca, graffiti of a distinctly adult sort has been cropping up on gallery walls, condo halls. And the ranks of writers have lately been swelled by some of the same punkers who can be seen puking it up on Avenue A. Keith Haring, whose potent glyphs grace sidewalks and subways alike in lower Manhattan, seems to have spawned a generation of art-school vandals. Their work bears less resemblance to Wild Style (as the most ambitious graffiti of recent years is often called) than to concrete poetry and its nexus with visual art via the St. Marks school.

Cryptic texts have replaced the underground creati-vity; the mode of execution is less free-hand and more precise; materials include not just spray paint but elaborate stencils; and the placement of these more modest "masterpieces" is often camouflaged, sacrificing confrontation for surprise — the salient mode of postconceptual art.

There's the rub: for if graffiti isn't confrontational, is it graffiti? What with many young masters shifting into career modes of their own, they may be too busy to cast aspersions on the new graffiti-punks. In any event, it's fair solace to slide into adulthood knowing you've created a style, even if the first manifestation of middle age is the contempt you feel for what it has become. New Wave graffiti makes it that much harder to ignore the aesthetic potential of the stuff, that much harder to mount a multimillion-dollar public-relations campaign against it. And in the process of adapting the strategies of Wild Style, artists are helping to assimilate writers from the ghetto into an increasingly rich avant-soup.

At this point, receptivity to graffiti is the difference between uptown and downtown sensibilities. As one New Wave artist recently remarked, "It's our reggae."

Richard Goldstein

Afterword

I visited Martha Cooper in the autumn of 2004. She showed me her photographic archive and produced a handful of pictures from a file drawer marked tags and placed them on the lightbox. Knockout. Here they were, hundreds of pictures of very early tags.

In Sweden, I have followed the wall scribblings since I learned to read. They were a way to check on names and messages from one part of town to another. The names became mythical, my own private Olympus. New ones constantly appeared and were seldom removed: in pedestrian tunnels, at bus stops, in the subway or swimming pool changing rooms. Then graffiti came to Europe in 1984. I started writing tags when I was twelve, and haven't been able to stop. Writing tags is the most relaxing and creative activity I know.

When I returned to New York in the winter of 2007, we sat in Martha's studio for four days. I sorted slides and she scanned them. Every morning I was met by her friendly cats and the good news that she had found new pictures and articles in her bottomless archive. We took the subway to Washington Heights and searched for the rocks and bridge supports in High Bridge Park that Martha had photographed in 1981. We found old Baby Face 86 tags in Riverside Park and discussed the title of the book with Mare 139 and Ket and heard tagging tales from Blade.

Jacob Kimvall visited New York in the spring of 2007 and looked at the pictures together with Part 1. Part shared his rich experience as did Snake 1, with whom Jacob went to the 188th Street Writers' Corner. The generously shared knowledge of these legends has been indispensable to the creation of *Tag Town*.

At last, the world can experience these unique images. They can be discussed, evaluated, analyzed and may inspire new generations of writers. The earliest writers may be sought out and interviewed. The scholars of the tag world can press the record button and start their work. It won't be over in the foreseeable future.

Martha Cooper's photographs provide a keyhole for us to look through and experience New York graffiti's infancy, something for which all of us who were not privileged to experience it firsthand are deeply grateful.

Tobias Barenthin Lindblad
Stockholm, Sweden

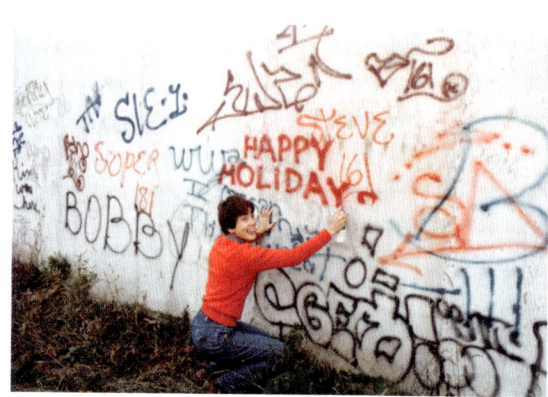

Martha Cooper preparing a greeting card in 1976.

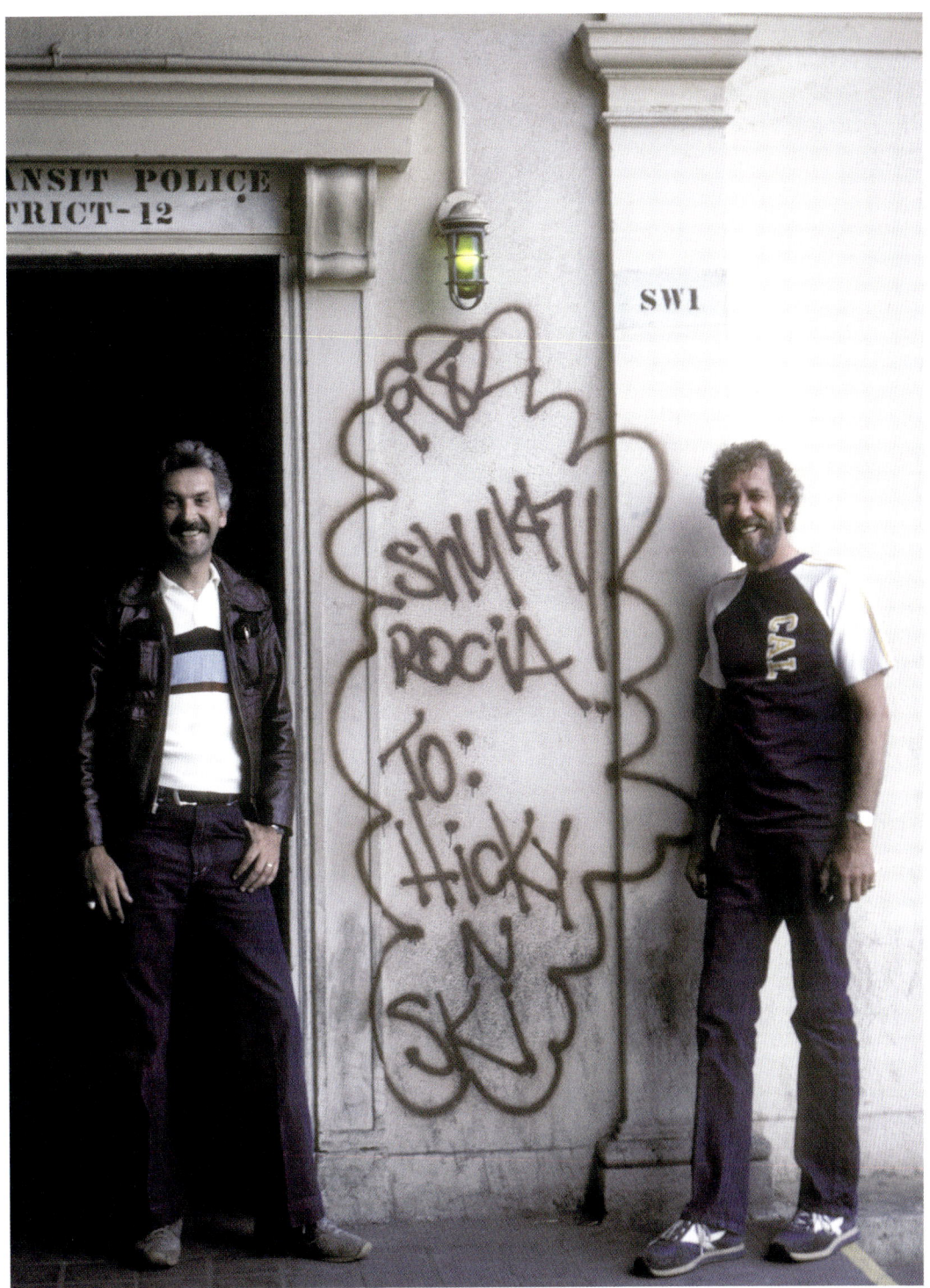

Hickey and Ski, legendary Vandal Squad cops with Shy 147's tribute.

Bios & Bibliography

Martha Cooper was one of the first photographers to document the culture of graffiti. The photos in her first book, *Subway Art* (1984), with Henry Chalfant have inspired generations of graffiti writers worldwide. At present, Cooper is a freelance photographer specializ-ing in urban life. Her books include *R.I.P.: Memorial Wall Art* (1994), *Hip Hop Files* (2004), *We B* Girlz* (2005), *Street Play* (2006), *New York State of Mind* (2007) and *Tokyo Tattoo 1970* (2011). She is based in Manhattan.

Blade is one of the great graffiti kings who painted the New York subway for fifteen years. A member of the crew The Crazy Five, he created 5.000 pieces from 1972 to 1984. He is known throughout the world for his original style. Florida is his home where he paints on canvas and exhibits his work internationally.

Part I is a veteran of the New York graffiti scene. As a member of the all-star group The Death Squad, he was an innovative stylist during the 1970s. Part is still active as an artist, and an important contributor to the New York mural scene.

Snake I was one of the most active graffiti writers at the 188th Street Writers' Corner in Washington Heights. With his friend Stitch 1, he was also a member of the organization United Graffiti Artists. Snake gave up graffiti when he left Manhattan in 1974.

Tobias Barenthin Lindblad started writing graffiti in 1988 in his home town of Stockholm. He works as an author, archivist and editor at Dokument Press. Tobias is a dedicated lecturer and organizes graffiti workshops in Sweden and abroad.

In our work with *Tag Town,* these sources were useful:

Castleman, Craig: **Getting Up – Subway Graffiti in New York**, MIT Press 1982 *A comprehensive introduction to the culture of graffiti with excellent interviews with major New York writers.*

Chalfant, Henry & Cooper, Martha: **Subway Art**, Thames & Hudson 1984. *The classic graffiti book, called* The Bible *by writers.*

Fedorchak, Vincent: **Fuzz One**, Testify Books 2005. *A fascinating first person account of a writer's life and exploits in early 70s New York.*

Kimvall, Jacob: **Bortom klichéerna – om graffiti och den samtida konstens gränser**, Stockholm University 2007. *A thesis in Art History that examines the relationship between graffiti and institutionalized art. In Swedish.*

Kohl, Herbert & Hinton, James: **Golden Boy as Anthony Kool**, Dial Press 1972. *A ground-breaking study of New York graffiti in the 60s.*

Kurlansky, Mervyn; Mailer, Norman & Naar, Jon: **The Faith of Graffiti**, Alskog & Praeger 1974. *A beautiful book with photos of early subway graffiti and cultural commentary by Norman Mailer.*

Public Wall Writing in Philadelphia, Free News Project 2006. *Archival photos of early Philly graffiti.*

Stewart, Jack: **Subway Graffiti. An Aesthetic Study of Graffiti on the Subway System of New York City, 1970–1978**, New York University 1989. *A thorough study of early subway graffiti.*

Plakins Thornton, Tamara: **Handwriting in America – A cultural history**, Yale University Press 1996. *An informative book about penmanship in the U.S.*

Wonder, Stevie: **Down to Earth**, Tamla, Detroit 1966.

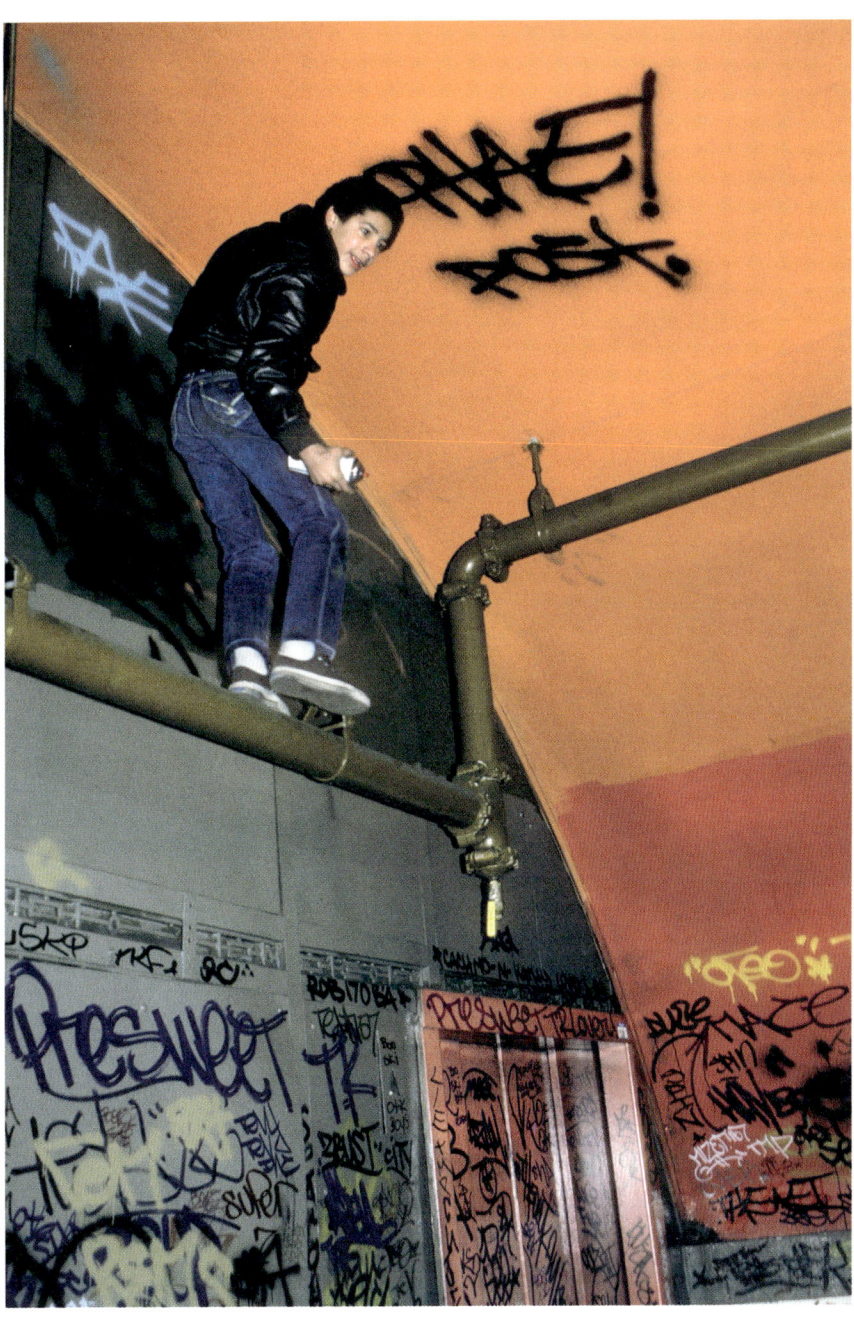

Writing your name identifies who you are. The more you write your name, the more you begin to think about and the more you begin to be about who you are. Once you start doing that, you start to assert your individualism and when you do that, you have an identity.

Wicked Gary
from *Getting Up* by Craig Castleman.

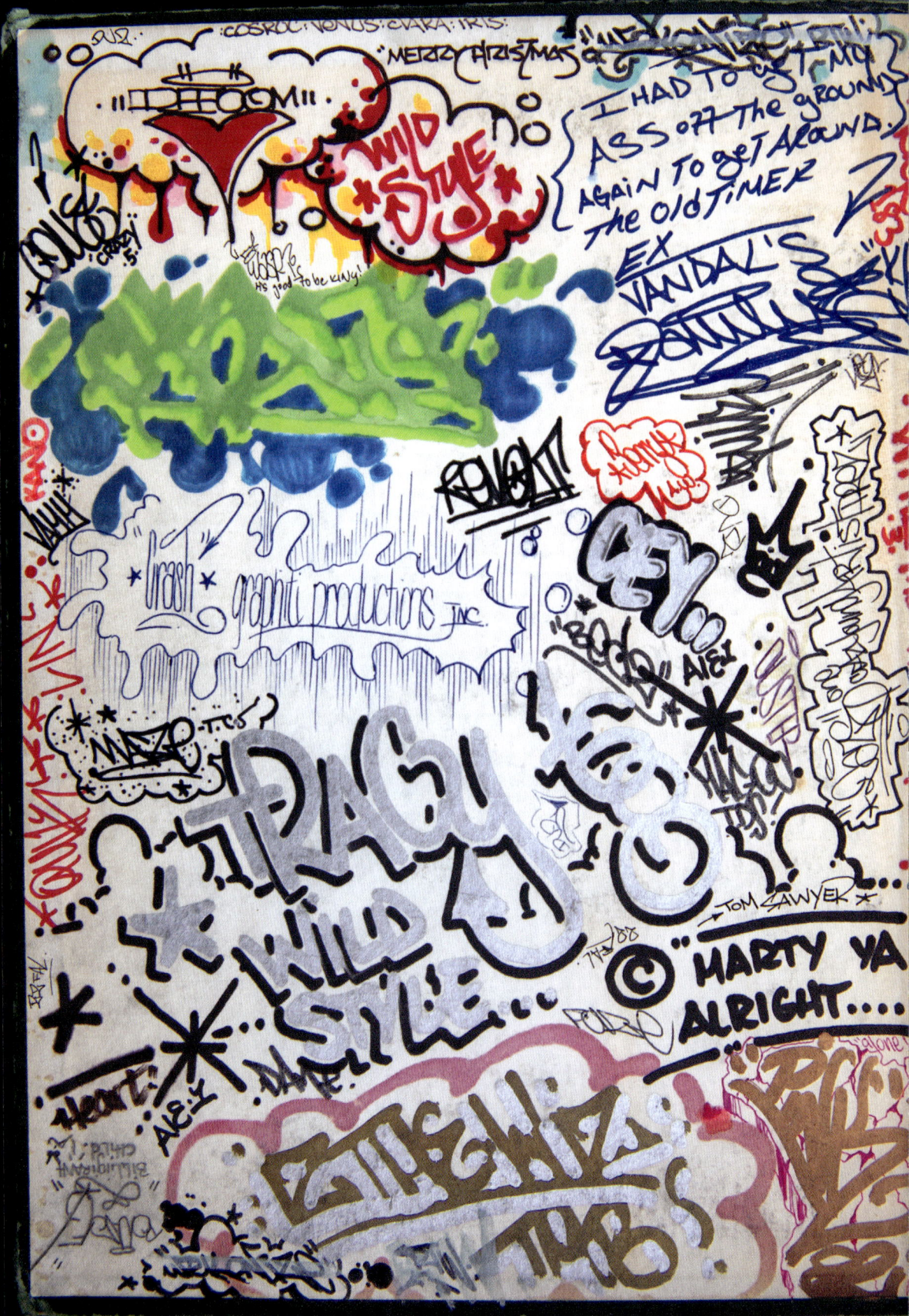

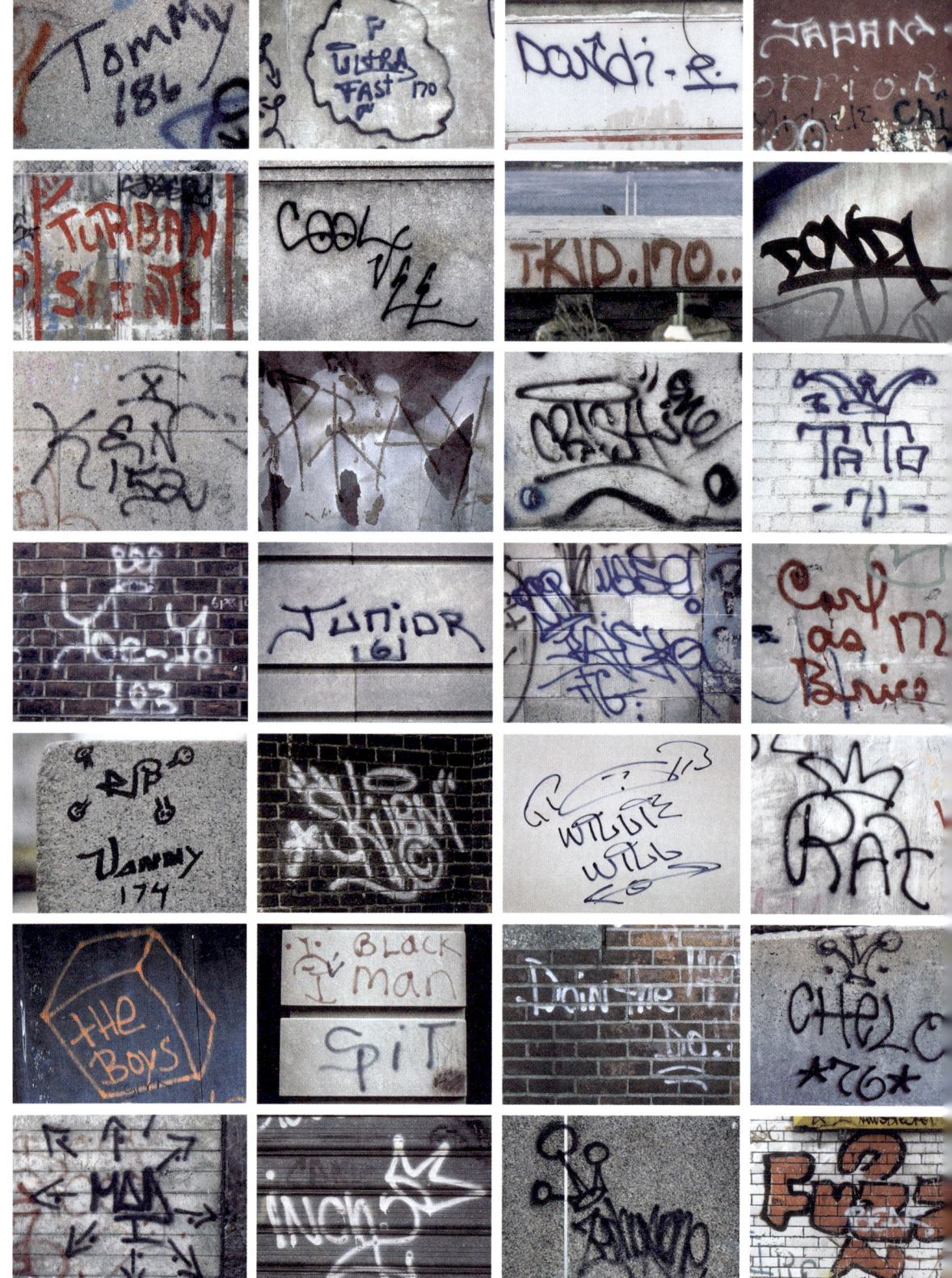